Entrepreneurship and Innovation Education

To Baptiste, Maia, Léa and Louise,
may their visions and plans come true

To Sylvie, constant source of inspiration.

Smart Innovation Set

coordinated by
Dimitri Uzunidis

Volume 32

Entrepreneurship and Innovation Education

Frameworks and Tools

Marcos Lima

iSTE

WILEY

First published 2020 in Great Britain and the United States by ISTE Ltd and John Wiley & Sons, Inc.

ISTE Ltd
27-37 St George's Road
London SW19 4EU
UK

www.iste.co.uk

John Wiley & Sons, Inc.
111 River Street
Hoboken, NJ 07030
USA

www.wiley.com

Library of Congress Control Number: 2020945629

British Library Cataloguing-in-Publication Data
A CIP record for this book is available from the British Library
ISBN 978-1-78630-622-7

MIX
Paper from responsible sources
FSC® C013604

Contents

Introduction

This book is a compilation of practical insights for entrepreneurship and innovation (E&I) education based on tools, techniques and frameworks I have developed or adopted in my 20-year career as a teacher. As most of this experience took place in France, my country of adoption, the book is biased towards a European perspective of this phenomenon. However, its applicability is by no means restricted to this continent – it could be adopted anywhere in the world.

Why write another book about entrepreneurship and innovation education? As mentioned above, this book is focused on creating a "toolbox" of frameworks for analyzing entrepreneurship and innovation problems and making decisions. Like my previous books (Lima and Fabiani 2014, 2016), this one assumes that the human brain cannot articulate more than three or four dimensions of a problem without the aid of what might be called "checklists for thinking": frameworks (visual or otherwise) that help students think in terms of multiple variables affecting a problem. A typical example of a very valuable tool for thinking about business creation is the Business Model Canvas by Alexander Osterwalder and Yves Pigneur (2010). It suggests nine building blocks to think about how value is created, delivered and captured throughout the process. Before this framework was proposed, students of entrepreneurship and innovation tended to focus either on the value creation or on the value delivery process, or neglected to contemplate the relationship between the multiple dimensions involved. Thus, I strongly believe that one of the main roles of a business educator is to provide students with a toolbox for analyzing different problems using appropriate concepts, preferably in a visual manner. This manual presents an extensive list of frameworks and analytical models that can be used in different stages of entrepreneurship and innovation education. As Abraham Maslow is believed to have said, "If all you have in your head is a hammer, every problem looks like a nail." Appendix 1 lists all the frameworks used in the book for easy reference.

Furthermore, the book introduces the notion of "collaborative interactivity" as a mediating principle to teaching and learning innovation and entrepreneurship. This principle is drawn from my PhD thesis (summarized in English in Lima *et al.* 2004). It explores how the constructivist approach of "learning by doing" can enhance knowledge acquisition through a combination of reflection, interaction and collaboration in a real-life setting. At the end of most chapters, a "teaching and learning" section illustrates how I have applied these principles in my own classes, often relying on collaborative technologies and cloud-based resources to enhance student interaction and engagement. Chapter 1 discusses these principles and how they are applied in more depth.

Another important characteristic of this book is its emphasis on a more dynamic strategic view of business model innovation based on the principles of effectuation (Sarasvathy 2001) and human-centric innovation (such as Business Model Design, Customer Development, Design Thinking and Lean Startup). Many business schools in Europe still prompt entrepreneurship students to write long business plans, often based on dangerously flawed assumptions. We build a case in this book on how a more dynamic approach, based on business model testing and product or service prototyping, is a much more effective way of learning about real innovation opportunities. This does not mean that old-school business planning should be buried and forgotten. Indeed, the initial chapters of this book discuss typical business plan structures and the analytical tools involved in moving from vision to plan. Even though the effectuation approaches discussed in later chapters have proven to be more adapted to the dynamic nature of entrepreneurship and innovation projects, static business plans could be a good starting point to gain an overview of the initial strategic elements, which may help mature the entrepreneur's vision. The problem with these plans, we argue, is their tendency to become a static reference point for every decision beyond the initial stages of vision development. This danger must be avoided by applying dynamic effectuation approaches such as business modeling and design thinking.

I.1. A humble contribution to strengthening entrepreneurship and innovation in Europe

One of the challenges of writing a book about E&I in Europe is that there are multiple perspectives on a continent so culturally diverse. We do not have the pretension of presenting "the" definitive and comprehensive view of this phenomenon for the continent, but simply "a" perspective from my own experience of teaching European students for over a decade in France.

To illustrate how differently E&I are perceived in Europe, Dodd *et al.* (2013) analyzed positive and negative metaphors associated with entrepreneurs in a continent-wide survey. Whereas 46% of Greeks had a negative attitude towards entrepreneurs (blood-sucking leeches), in Ireland 82.3% saw them positively (bright and illuminating rainbows). Table I.1 presents these differences.

Positive images	
% per country	Predominant metaphor
Ireland (82.3%)	Bright and illuminating rainbows
The Netherlands (73.8%)	Lubricating oil of economy
UK (72.5%)	Poets. They must invent new ideas and turn them into something profitable
Italy (70%)	The wings of freedom
Cyprus (65.5%)	A ship with a good captain. They know where the ship begins its voyage and where it docks. They have targets
Poland (49.3%)	Hunters – they are persistent on their aspirations for a success
Greece (41%)	Conductors of the orchestra
Negative images	
% per country	Predominating metaphor
Greece (46%)	Leeches, because they suck the blood of the employees
Poland (26.2%)	Stone – insensitive to the needs of others
Italy (20.7%)	Leeches
Cyprus (20.5%)	Foxes – they try to sell their products in a treacherous way
UK (13.5%)	The historical titanic, the discovery shuttle
Ireland (7.3%)	Hares, running about all over the place
The Netherlands (5.7%)	Profiteer

Table I.1. *Different perceptions about entrepreneurs across Europe (adapted from Dodd* et al. *2013)*

If the tools adopted in Europe are the same that are being used in Silicon Valley, creating a new venture in the Old World remains a much harder exercise. According to Henrekson and Sanandaji (2018), Europe overall has an "entrepreneurship deficit" that is largely acknowledged in the public debate. We have a less dense institutional framework for innovation and the venture capital sector is less developed. Europe has fewer innovative firms and lower R&D efforts among startups.

Wright *et al.* (2007) show that whereas in the USA we have 140 adults per 10,000 in nascent ventures with an expectation of having more than 19 employees in the next five years, this number is much lower for European countries: 70 in the UK, 49 in Sweden, 46 in Germany, 38 in France and 16 in Belgium. This is not just a matter of creating startups, but also scaling them up. Table I.2 shows the number of large firms founded since 1990 in the USA, China and Europe, depicting the vast superiority of the Americans in this domain.

	Billionaire entrepreneurs per million	**Number of startups valued at 1B+ (unicorns)**	**Large firms founded since 1990**
USA	1.37	115	60
China	0.17	47	22
East Asia	0.55	8	19
Eastern Europe	0.13	1	2
Western Europe	0.47	22	18
Germany	0.52	5	3
UK	0.72	10	5
France	0.39	2	1
Italy	0.38	0	1
Spain	0.26	0	1
Nordic	0.62	2	0
Switzerland	1.75	1	2
Canada	1.06	2	3
Israel	1.75	2	1

Table I.2. *Entrepreneurship and value creation in different countries (adapted from Henrekson and Sanandaji 2018)*

This book is thus a humble attempt to contribute to narrowing this gap by sharing with teachers and students of E&I in Europe up-to-date tools and methods more widely used by the most dynamic startup clusters in the USA, by applying teaching and learning approaches based on constructivist principles.

I.2. A note about entrepreneurship versus innovation education

Our text treats entrepreneurship and innovation interchangeably, even though we are aware of the obvious differences between creating a new venture (which does not necessarily involve innovation) and improving the value creation process (which does not necessarily involve entrepreneurship). This conscious choice was made for the sake of enlarging the audience of the book, as several of the entrepreneurship tools used for creating new ventures can be adapted to innovation projects of "intrapreneurship". Conversely, every entrepreneur who wishes to grow their business must become familiar with innovation tools.

I.3. Who is this book for?

This guide targets entrepreneurship and innovation teachers looking for proven tools to facilitate the process of new venture creation according to the pedagogical principles of Collaborative Interactivity, enriched with digital support systems and project-based learning. At the end of each chapter, professors will find a summary of teaching and learning strategies adapted to each stage of the entrepreneurship and innovation (E&I) process, with examples of best practices extracted either from my own experience or that of other E&I teachers.

The book was also conceived for students of E&I courses interested in hands-on tools for developing new businesses. The text presents over 50 frameworks as it follows the stages of new venture creation: how to go from a vague idea to a clearer vision, how to transform the vision into a business plan and then how to transform this static plan into a testable, dynamic business model strategy. They will then learn how to apply Design Thinking principles to prototype their products and services and how to test and improve them before they start their businesses. We conclude by presenting the challenges of keeping the business innovative as it scales up.

Finally, this guide can also be used by "intrapreneurs". This type of innovative entrepreneur consists, according to Schumpeter (1982), of managers who have the will and the power to perform the "entrepreneurial function" in companies or startups they do not own. Indeed, the tools and methods described here can be applied both to new venture creation and to mature business development. By better understanding the unmet needs of existing or new customers, intrapreneurs can use this guide to fulfill them with more innovative products, services and business models.

Maybe we should also alert readers to what this book is *not*. It is not a detailed manual on how to use the dozens of frameworks presented here. It is meant as a summary overview of the "forest" of tools available to teachers and students of entrepreneurship and innovation, not a guide on how to apply them in detail. The internet (as well as our own references at the end of the book) contains several resources to go deeper on each tool, depending on the reader's interests and needs. Thus, the text was kept deliberately short to make the reader aware of the different approaches to developing visionary products and services, and how to learn and teach them, without getting lost in the details. Once the contours of the "forest" are well understood from this "helicopter perspective", it is much easier to descend onto the "canopy" and explore specific "trees".

1

E&I Education: An Overview[1]

This chapter defines the nature of entrepreneurship and innovation, as well as the limits and possibilities for teaching and learning the skills involved. It discusses some of the differences between traditional management education and training versus E&I-focused programs. It briefly argues the eternal question of whether entrepreneurship can be taught. It presents a framework for understanding the E&I education landscape and some of the processes and expected outputs of this educational system. It illustrates this approach with a case of a French University E&I education program. Finally, it presents the Collaborative Interactivity approach to teaching and learning E&I.

This section is designed to help professors to better understand some of the challenges of E&I teaching. It is highly theoretical and should be of little interest to students. If you are a student, we suggest you skip this section entirely and go straight to Chapter 2, about how to develop your entrepreneurship vision.

1.1. Defining entrepreneurship and innovation

The phenomenon of entrepreneurship lacks a single, universally accepted definition (Valerio *et al.* 2014). Kirzner (1999) defines it as a process of identifying and exploring (frequently unnoticed) profit opportunities. Klapper *et al.* (2010) describe it simply as the process of creating new

1 Parts of this chapter have been adapted from our article published with Albertini, Thierry and Lameta about a Framework for Evaluating Entrepreneurship Education (Albertini *et al.* 2019).

wealth. In its narrowest definition, entrepreneurship is *the process of converting ideas into products or services and then creating a new venture to market it* (Johnson 2001). Innovation, on the other hand, can be simply defined as "the process of turning opportunity into new ideas and of putting these into widely used practice" (Tidd and Bessant 2013, p. 19). As can be seen from the definitions above, E&I are intrinsically correlated. Creating new ventures does not necessarily imply innovating and, conversely, one may be an innovator without creating a new business. Nevertheless, it can be argued that the kind of entrepreneurship that creates most value does involve innovation. As Peter Drucker (1994) suggested, innovation is the main tool of entrepreneurs.

Joseph Schumpeter's view of this phenomenon is widely accepted as one of the most relevant and comprehensive to date. According to this Austrian economist who pioneered the field, an entrepreneur is someone involved in the creation of innovative and growth-pursuing firms (Schumpeter 1982). He argues that innovative companies grow faster by introducing new goods or new methods of production, by opening new markets, by conquering of new sources of supply and by carrying out a new organization of an industry. These categories are the basis for the standardized types of innovation as defined by the *Oslo Manual for Collecting and Interpreting Innovation Data* (OECD 2005): product innovation, process innovation, marketing innovation and organizational innovation.

Let us examine each of the Schumpeterian categories below.

– **New products or services**. Arguably the most visible part of innovation, this process consists of identifying unmet customer needs and developing solutions that deliver superior value. Superior value can be achieved by designing products and services that offer better quality, more convenience, lower cost or any other differentiation attribute that is valued by the target customer. An example of this kind of innovation would be a more effective toothpaste, a less expensive computer or a better designed customer experience.

– **New methods of production**. Also known as process innovation, this approach consists of improving existing methods to lower costs, increase efficiency, lower environmental impact or achieve any other enhancement in the way products and services are created and delivered. Examples of this type of innovation could include improving the quality, reducing the cost or increasing the speed of a project, or reducing the amount of wood used in the manufacturing of furniture.

– **Opening new markets, foreign or domestic**. Contrary to widespread belief, an innovation does not have to be "new". If an existing product, service or process is introduced in a new market segment which was previously unfamiliar with its benefits, this can be considered an innovation in the Schumpeterian perspective. Examples include successfully introducing a gaming console targeting non-gamers or introducing an old product in new country or region.

– **Conquering new sources of supply**. This is about working with suppliers to adopt materials or energy source with better performance, lower cost or improved environmental impact. An example would consist of contributing to the transition towards a fossil-fuel-free society.

– **Carrying out a new organization of an industry**. This final Schumpeterian category is the most difficult to achieve and most powerful type of innovation. It consists of introducing such innovative products or services or using such revolutionary methods of production that the rules of the game in an entire economic sector are changed. Ford's use of the assembly line to produce affordable cars in the early 20th Century is another example. So was Toyota's introduction of its total quality movement in the 1980s. The introduction of personal computers in the 1980s or smartphones in the 2000s are instances of this powerful disruption.

The entrepreneurship definitions by Schumpeter assume that innovation is an intrinsic part of value creation. It does not exclude the phenomenon of "intrapreneurship" (Drucker 1994), that is, a manager who innovates in one of the above categories without necessarily owning shares in the firm. Like Schumpeter and Drucker, we believe that the entrepreneurship spirit could and should be part of any manager's attributes, and that is the reason why intrapreneurs are the third target of this book.

According to this approach, it is not enough to create a new venture to be considered an entrepreneur. One must innovate. In our understanding, innovation is *the process of addressing the unmet needs of a large enough group of people to sustain a business or organization*. This definition is compatible with Schumpeter's view without requiring radical or entirely new products, services or business models. Indeed, being first to market may result in failure to innovate.

To illustrate this underlying principle, let us take the case of one of the most innovative companies of the last decades: Apple. They have created what can be arguably considered one of the largest value-yielding empires in the history of mankind without ever having been "first to market". They did not launch the first personal computer, the first portable music player, the first smartphone, the first tablet or the first smartwatch. But when they did launch each one of these groundbreaking product categories, they took deep care to address the unmet needs of a large audience, whether that need was user-friendliness, integration or elegant design.

Therefore, for the purposes of this book, innovation and entrepreneurship are profoundly intertwined. True entrepreneurship in the Schumpeterian sense requires more than simply creating a business: we must constantly try to understand and serve the ever-evolving needs of customers by launching better products or services, by improving our processes and by opening up new markets or segments. On the other hand, innovating in a well-established business is as important as creating new ones. Thus, the tools and insights offered in this book are also valuable to intrapreneurs.

1.2. Innovation and entrepreneurship education

Valerio *et al.* (2014) make a distinction between entrepreneurship and business management education. Typically, in a European business school, business management focuses on two key competencies: corporate management and enterprise development. In their first year of management, students are often exposed to the principles of organizational theory and its foundational sciences (psychology and sociology) while developing hard skills associated with corporate finance (based on financial mathematics) and accounting, risk management (including notions of statistics and probability), macro- and micro-economics. As this underlying knowledge is acquired, students are better prepared to understand organizational development, having disciplines such as strategic planning, innovation management, sales, marketing and accounting later in the program. Entrepreneurship education builds upon these competencies of enterprise development while adding specific disciplines about softer, "socio-emotional" skills, such as creativity, entrepreneurial vision, business model design, product management and business planning (Figure 1.1).

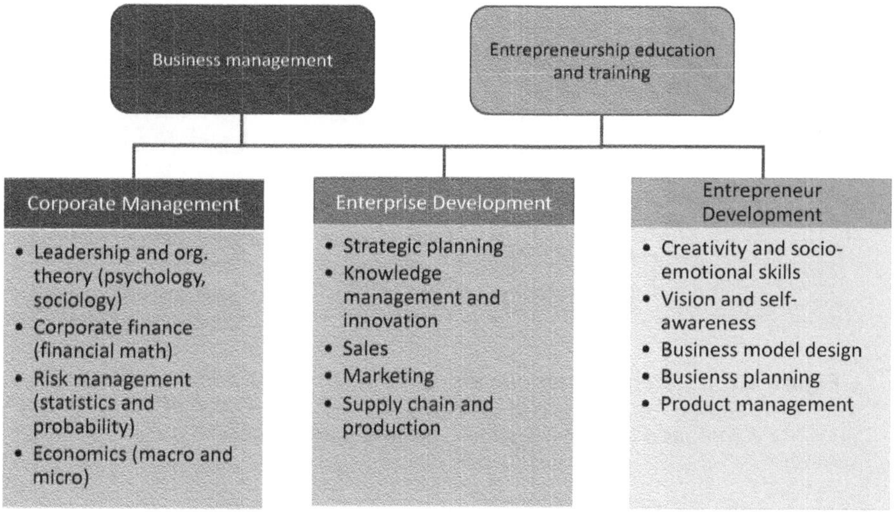

Figure 1.1. *Business management versus entrepreneurship education (adapted from Valerio* et al. *2014). For a color version of the figure, see http://www.iste.co.uk/lima/entrepreneurship.zip*

Valerio *et al.* (2014) make a further distinction between entrepreneurship *education* (within the context of secondary and higher education institutions) and entrepreneurship *training* (for people outside the regular education system). Training programs are often offered by European governments to vulnerable, unemployed individuals in the hope of helping them create a self-employment business. Businesses created by these individuals are seldom innovative in nature. However, a second type of individual often seeks entrepreneurship training programs: inspired professionals who come across an opportunity to innovate. Training programs are also offered to active small business owners who wish to hone their entrepreneurship skills. Government-funded training programs hope to transform uninspired individuals into active innovators and regular SMB owners into developers of high-growth businesses (see Figure 1.2).

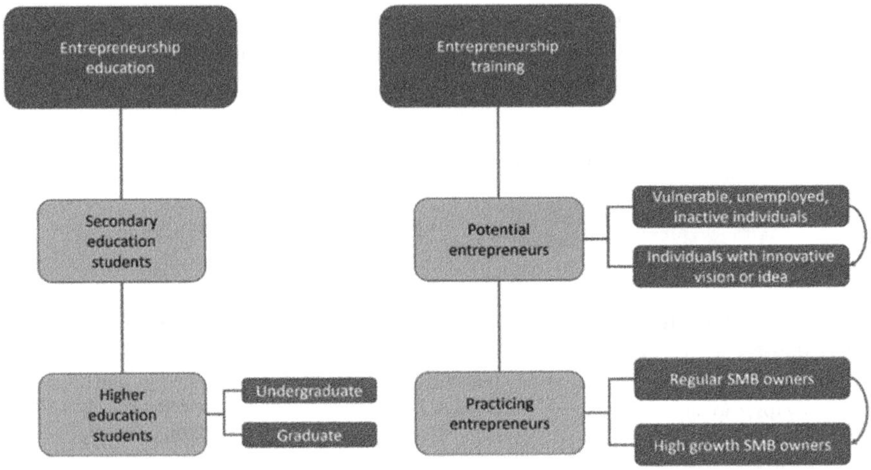

Figure 1.2. *Differences between entrepreneurship education and training (adapted from Valerio* et al. *2014). For a color version of the figure, see http://www.iste.co.uk/lima/entrepreneurship.zip*

These definitions and examples illustrate the main challenges involved in teaching entrepreneurship and innovation in the 21st Century. The speed of digital transformation has multiplied the tools to prototype product and service design, to create more efficient processes, to reach new markets beyond the barriers of time and space and to create entirely new business models, as the examples of Uber and AirBnB illustrate. In order to keep up with this transformation, students must experiment with in-class digital tools that facilitate self-learning, collaborating and sharing projects in a real-world setting.

There is a European consensus about the importance of teaching E&I. According to Fayolle and Gailly (2008, p. 572),

> A recent work conducted by a European group of experts representing all EU member countries proposed a common definition [of entrepreneurship education]. The consensus reached led to the inclusion of two distinct elements: (1) A broader concept of entrepreneurship education which should include the development of entrepreneurial attitudes and skills as well as personal qualities and which should not be directly focused on the creation of new ventures; and (2) A more

> specific concept of new venture creation-oriented training (European Commission 2002).

We argue that in order to foster relevant "attitudes and skills" mentioned in the first part of this definition, we should include a series of digital tools and project-based learning approaches explored in this book. Rather than simply consider this as a process of "knowledge transfer" concerning opportunities to created new products and services (Hindle 2007), we propose a constructivist approach in which future entrepreneurs, intrapreneurs and innovators build their own knowledge from the practice of project-based activities. Indeed, the word "teaching" hardly seems appropriate in this process. As Fayolle and Gailly (2008, p. 574) further argue:

> Given that entrepreneurship refers rather to individual initiative, creativity and sometimes innovation, it appears inadequate to favor the emergence of entrepreneurs or make a society more entrepreneurial by only giving lessons or "imparting knowledge". In the definition proposed above, teaching appears to imply a degree of passivity from the learner. The word "educate" seems therefore more appropriate. Indeed, entrepreneurship education relates to the evolution of learning processes and methods from a didactical mode towards an entrepreneurial mode.

If Europe wishes to catch up with the USA in terms of entrepreneurship and innovation dynamics, it must start by appreciating the difference between E&I teaching and education. The latter implicates developing critical and creative thinking in the learner's minds, whereas the former is based on lecture-centric approach that is less and less relevant as students can find information and tools by their own resources given the wealth of Internet media (massive open online courses or MOOCs, YouTube tutorials, social media discussion forums and the plethora of websites dedicated to the theme). That is not to say that instructional lectures are completely irrelevant. If operational "know-how" and higher-level "know-how-to-think critically and creatively" are the ultimate goals, it is also important to assure declarative knowledge ("know what" and "know why") as a basis for intellectual autonomy. Thus, we do not suggest eliminating traditional teaching altogether but enriching it with more participative, bottom-up learning processes. Overall, we must not confuse ideal methods for teaching entrepreneurship and innovation with those traditionally used for management education, both in terms of contents and form (Johnson *et al,* 2006). When teaching entrepreneurship, professors must adopt the role and attitude of a facilitator and advisor rather than that of an instructor (Lautenschläger and Haase 2011). As Hills (1988) suggested (after looking into the attitudes of 15 of the most recognized American entrepreneurship teachers), entrepreneurship mentors must act and feel “entrepreneurial”. This has not always been the case: Bennett (2006) conducted a study of 141 teachers in entrepreneurship in England, concluding that many of them lacked entrepreneurship experience, reflecting on their traditional approaches to teaching the subject. These deficiencies can and should be compensated by specific teacher training programs aimed at giving them more direct involvement with the process of new venture creation.

1.3. Can entrepreneurship be taught? Towards a framework of E&I education

Since the first entrepreneurship courses were introduced in Harvard Business School in the 1940s, there has been a longstanding debate on whether entrepreneurship can be taught. Akola and Heinonen (2006) distinguish between the “art” and the “science” of entrepreneurship. According to them, the soft skills involved (e.g. creativity, innovative thinking) cannot be learned in school, they require practical experience. The “scientific knowledge”, however (e.g. business and management skills), can be taught.

This distinction seems rather artificial in our experience. Tacit knowledge involved in soft skills are indeed harder to teach, but active learning pedagogical approaches discussed in this book could help students experience “real-life” scenarios in the classroom. By applying concepts and frameworks to relevant situations and collaborating in small groups, we have experienced how students can become more creative, critical thinkers while developing better communication, negotiation and leadership skills. Thus, we fully agree with Peter Drucker (1994) that E&I can be presented as a discipline, which can both be learned and practiced. The issue therefore is not “whether” E&I can be taught or learned, but “how”.

Lautenshläger and Haase (2011) list a series of barriers to entrepreneurship and innovation education, such as the lack of uniform objectives and pedagogical content, overemphasis on the "traits of successful entrepreneurs" and the difficulty to measure impact on students. Fiet (2001) further argues that it is unlikely that students will face the same scenarios that teachers use in class to contextualize their concepts and that ideal entrepreneurial behavior examples from great innovators could actually have a "demoralizing" effect on aspiring students (who may feel they are "no Steve Jobs").

While all of these are real difficulties faced by entrepreneurship and innovation educators, we argue in this book that with an appropriate E&I educational framework, most of these barriers can be minimized or overcome. In this sense, Pittaway and Cope (2007) propose a general overview of the fundamental elements that must be present in a healthy relationship between entrepreneurship education institutions and the overall business ecosystem (Figure 1.3).

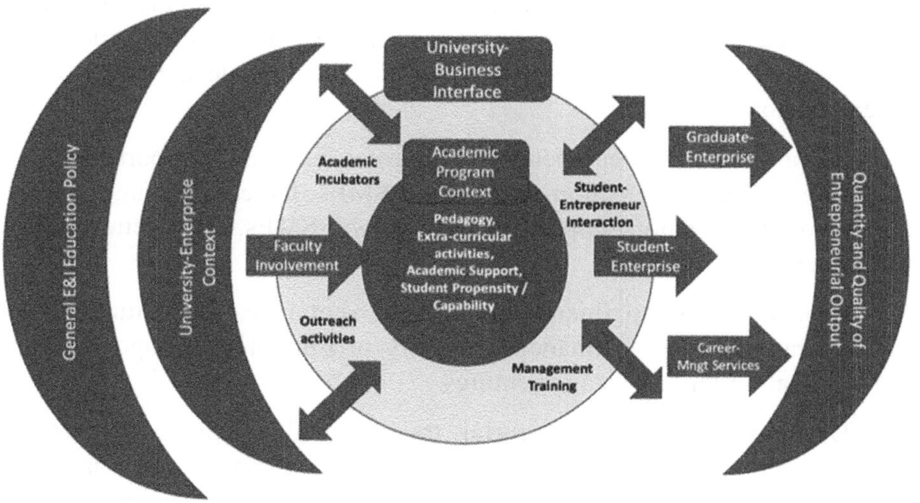

Figure 1.3. *University–enterprise interface and the entrepreneurial ecosystem (adapted from Pittaway and Cope 2007). For a color version of the figure, see http://www.iste.co.uk/lima/entrepreneurship.zip*

Pittaway and Cope's framework can be read from left to right in terms of a basic input–process–output system. The starting point and one of the key elements of the European entrepreneurship ecosystem are the general E&I education policies from the regional and national governments. According to the "Entrepreneurship 2020 Action Plan"[2] by the European Commission (published in 2012), the following topics were considered a priority expectation of European governments by entrepreneurs and business support organizations in the ecosystem:

– Streamline new venture creation processes – reduce the number of administrative procedures, avoid duplication of tasks, speed up and simplify licensing and permits, optimize tax systems, increase social protection for entrepreneurs, raise awareness of government administrations about SME challenges, improve the quality and variety of government services for startups.

– Facilitate transfers of business – improve legal and tax provisions for business transfers, improve information services for potential business transfer stakeholders, develop marketplaces to facilitate business transfers.

– Develop more efficient bankruptcy procedures – give honest bankruptcies a second chance, develop or expand mentor programs to second starters, create more affordable procedures for business failure procedures, raise awareness against the stigmatization of failure, create specific financial incentives for second starters.

– Support new entrepreneurs – improve business support services, facilitate ecological transition for existing SMEs, increase training, finance and internationalization support for high growth SMEs, offer better support to business innovation.

– Improve access to finance – reinforce venture capital initiatives and loan guarantee, improve financial advisory of Enterprise Europe Network, reduce taxation for early stage ventures.

– Develop youth entrepreneurial training and education – create a European hub or platform for entrepreneurship learning and share best practices for content development, implementation and measurement, embed entrepreneurial attitudes and skills at all educational levels (primary, secondary, vocational, higher education networks), incentivize youth to have at least one entrepreneurial experience at secondary education stage, develop and share a common guiding framework to support the development of

2 Available at https://ec.europa.eu/docsroom/documents/10378/attachments/1/translations/en/renditions/pdf.

entrepreneurship education institutions, increase funding to entrepreneurial education via European education funding programs, increase entrepreneurial training.

Specific actions were also aimed at increasing entrepreneurship and innovation rates among women, seniors and minorities.

The second level of Pittaway and Cope's input phase is the "university-enterprise" context. We could "zoom into" this element using the Quadruple/Quintuple Helix frameworks developed by Carayannis *et al.* (2012) based on Etzkowitz and Leydesdorff's original Triple Helix model (2000). In their original work, Etkowitz and Leydesdorff argued that university-enterprise relations could not be understood outside of the ecosystem in which they take place. Such ecosystem consists, as we have seen, not only of companies and higher education institutions but also of government policies that foster entrepreneurship and innovation. Carayannis *et al.* (2012) develop this ecosystem even further, as depicted in Figure 1.4.

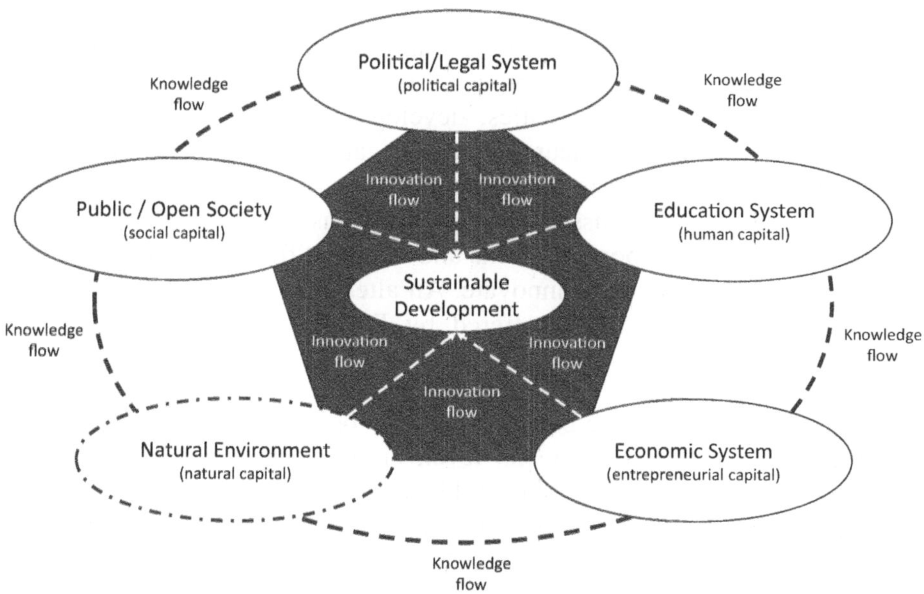

Figure 1.4. *The Quadruple/Quintuple Helix models (adapted from Carayannis* et al. *2012).*

According to this perspective, technology and knowledge are created both in universities (education system producing human capital) and in companies (economic system investing private capital, which in this chapter we designate as "entrepreneurship capital"). These, however, heavily rely on the incentives, disincentives and knowledge flows created not only by the government (political system with its policies, regulations and development programs) but also by the pressures of the public (media, NGOs, social institutions which provide legitimacy and trust through social capital) and the constraints from the natural environment (with increasing sustainability requirements).

Pittaway and Cope's framework captures well the political, human and entrepreneurial capital elements of the Quintuple Helix model but fails to mention the importance of civil society (social capital emanating from the institutions mentioned above) and the increasingly important natural capital. Indeed, one of the constraints of innovation and entrepreneurship in Europe in the 21st Century is the conciliation of economic development with sustainability.

At the heart of Pittaway and Cope's framework is the university–business interface. Leading into this process is the key factor of "faculty involvement" in outreach activities, development of academic incubation programs, student–entrepreneur interaction and basic managerial skills development. These efforts must be actively supported by the active pedagogy principles discussed in this book, as well as extracurricular activities, academic support programs and the identification of students with a high propensity/capacity to innovate. An alternative depiction of this core element in the framework is offered by Fayolle and Gailly (2008), as illustrated in Figure 1.5.

The authors differentiate between the ontological and educational levels of the problem. At the ontological level, before designing E&I programs, faculty members and other stakeholders (partners, government support agencies) should make sure they all agree on the meaning of entrepreneurship education, the adaptations that are necessary to the traditional education tools and the roles that each of them will play in this ecosystem. Then, at the educational level, we must understand the target audience, develop contents and methods adapted to that audience and establish clear metrics for assessment of skill acquisition by students.

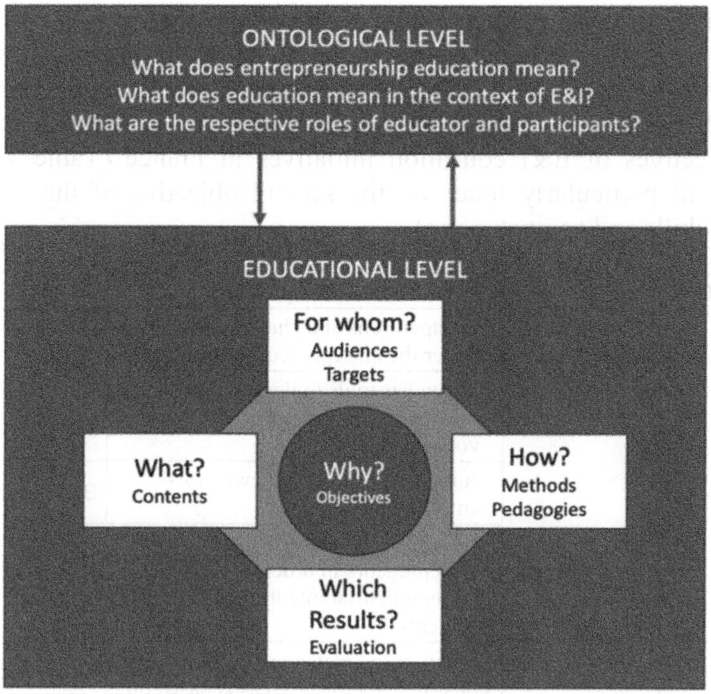

Figure 1.5. *Key questions in entrepreneurship education (adapted from Fayolle and Gailly 2008). For a color version of the figure, see http://www.iste.co.uk/lima/entrepreneurship.zip*

Concerning these skills, Valerio *et al.* (2014) argue that any E&I program should focus on developing self-confidence, leadership, creativity, risk propensity, motivation, resilience and self-efficacy. Students must be led to become aware of their affinity with E&I mindsets and competences, and they need to understand how their business knowledge and skills must be adapted to the process of new venture creation.

In a literature review of 108 articles about entrepreneurship education methods, Mwasalwiba (2010) found that the most common approach remains the use of presentations, videos and lectures (26 articles). However, more active learning methods were also very popular, such as (by decreasing frequency in the literature): case studies (12), group work (10), business simulations (10), business plan creation (8), real venture creation (6), games and competitions (6), project-based learning, workshops (6) and study visits (4).

This abundance and variety of active learning methods in E&I learning is a sign that most teachers in this domain realize the limitations of traditional lectures when trying to develop the necessary attitudes and skills in this domain. In our article with Albertini *et al.* (2019), we have categorized three main objectives of E&I education initiatives in France (Table 1.1). This chapter will particularly focus on the second objective of the framework (develop skills and competencies).

<table>
<tr><th colspan="2">Objectives</th><th>Examples</th><th>Academic studies</th></tr>
<tr><td colspan="2" rowspan="4">1. Raise awareness</td><td>Competitions and challenges to foster the entrepreneurial spirit</td><td>Arlotto et al. (2012)</td></tr>
<tr><td>Diagnosis tools to develop self-awareness and entrepreneurial vocation</td><td>Chené et al. (2011)</td></tr>
<tr><td>Junior enterprise – gateway to entrepreneurship</td><td>Barès et al. (2011)</td></tr>
<tr><td>Using guest lectures by star entrepreneurs in order to impact entrepreneurial intention among students</td><td>Boissin et al. (2007)</td></tr>
<tr><td rowspan="7">2. Develop skills and competencies</td><td rowspan="4">Pedagogical approaches</td><td>Action-based pedagogy designed to construct credible scenarios based on simple ideas</td><td>Filion et al. (2012)</td></tr>
<tr><td>Hybrid programs with both academic and professional courses</td><td>Verzat and Granger (2012)</td></tr>
<tr><td>Building an entrepreneurial pedagogy, based on four principles: empowering learners, providing first-hand experience, cooperative learning and reflective learning</td><td rowspan="2">Fayolle and Verzat (2009); Surlemont and Kearney (2009); Lima et al. (2004); Toutain (2011); Lima and Fabiani (2015)</td></tr>
<tr><td>Implement active teaching: the case method, problem-based learning and project-based teaching</td></tr>
<tr><td rowspan="3">Content</td><td>Adapt contents to student needs; highlight the generic objectives, targets, methods/teaching content and impact indicators</td><td>Bechard and Gregoire (2009); Mwasalwiba (2010)</td></tr>
<tr><td>Adopt a transversal, multidisciplinary and innovative approach; use creative methods to promote entrepreneurship</td><td>Sarow and Stuart (2013)</td></tr>
<tr><td>Teach ethical principles for socially responsible entrepreneurship</td><td>Fayolle and Toutain (2013)</td></tr>
</table>

Objectives		Examples	Academic studies
	Methods/ means	Focus training on the learner's ability to develop "know how"; using real-world situations to develop entrepreneurial competencies	Sarasvathy (2001); Aouni (2011)
		Substitute causal approaches (means to an end) by effectuation approaches (determining the possible effects based on the available means); relativize the power of predictive approaches and other myths about entrepreneur.	
		Stimulate taking risks in entrepreneurial situations ("situationist drift")	Dervaux (2011); Bureau and Fendt (2012)
		Bridging education and business worlds with experimental role-switching approaches such as "live my life"	
		Consider using innovative educational tools (use of videos, life stories, role plays, etc.)	Carrier (2009)
		Introductory classes to initiate students in the world of entrepreneurship and innovation	Toutain and Salgado (2015)
3. Provide support		Create a physical environment for developing entrepreneurial skills – incubator	Loué *et al.* (2008)
		Develop an entrepreneurial culture through networks: entrepreneurship hub, innovation support programs	Boissin and Schieb-Bienfait (2011)
		Establish a network of financial support (venture capitalists, angel investment programs, training on the use of crowdfunding platforms)	Lam (2010)

Table 1.1. *Examples of studies on the roles of entrepreneurship education in developing entrepreneurial intent (Albertini* et al. *2019)*

The pedagogical approaches listed in Table 1.1 are supposed to raise awareness, develop student vocation and improve their attitudes towards entrepreneurship (Boissin *et al.* 2007; Arlotto *et al.* 2012; Fayolle 2012). However, these initiatives often are fragmented (Verzat 2011) and confined within university walls, poorly connected with the entrepreneurial ecosystem (Verzat and Garant 2010). There have been attempts to integrate these initiatives in the main curriculum across European countries, creating a coherent approach to the content structure and how it is evaluated. The ultimate objective is to create a common background for evaluating and improving the quality of international entrepreneurial programs (Loué *et al.* 2008; Roeggiers 2012). Despite these attempts, a unified approach to evaluating the effectiveness of entrepreneurship programs remains an elusive ideal (Verzat and Granger 2012).

Some of these pedagogical approaches may seem confusing to both learners and teachers. Educational innovations often require a fresh mentality about the way we learn and teach, and resistances may appear from both sides of the fence (Verzat 2011). This resistance to change has several causes (Fayolle 2012): habit or inertia, fear of the unknown, perceived threats while facing new situations, denial, psychological stress, additional financial costs, hostility and perceived barriers from stakeholders. Indeed, entrepreneurship education should have a deep impact on attitudes if it is expected to change behavior; as such, it has sometimes been compared to a "cultural revolution" in teaching and learning (Chambard 2013). Furthermore, it must be noted that a good entrepreneurship program often may have the opposite effect on entrepreneurial intention: better knowledge of one's self, one's competencies and aptitudes may convince participants that they are *not* well suited to the entrepreneurship journey (Oosterbeek *et al.* 2010; Alis *et al.*, 2014).

Other factors may affect entrepreneurial intention. Timing, for instance: students who are closest to graduation (and who are therefore more clearly confronted with the prospect of a steady job) are more prone to cite obstacles to creating a new venture of their own (Boissin *et al.* 2009; Hallam *et al.* 2016). Another factor is the initial level of entrepreneurial intention before being exposed to a formal training (Fayolle and Gailly 2009). Hence, in order to develop a common framework about the efficacy of entrepreneurial programs, we must consider learning objectives, assessment methods, skills and attitudes (Hofer 2010; Verzat 2011). We must also take into account cultural implications, institutional and contextual variables – political, economic and social (Fayolle 2012). Universities must make the teaching of entrepreneurship relevant by emphasizing success stories of local SMEs; this requires close interaction with its territory, in particular through partnerships with local businesses. Such university–enterprise interactions are mutually beneficial and reinforce the role of universities as agents of regional development (Kitagawa 2005). In brief, we must build an "entrepreneurial education ecosystem" (Toutain *et al.* 2014).

Whereas traditional lectures are necessary to impart "know what", "know where" and "know who" and even "know why", constructivist methods are more adapted to develop "know how" competencies. In Mwasalwiba's survey (2010), the nine most frequent subjects in E&I were largely in this procedural knowledge domain: idea generation and opportunity discovery, business plan development, new venture creation process, risk management, marketing strategies, organization development, managing growth, finance and operational SME management.

1.3.1. *The French case*

According to the annual Global Entrepreneurship Monitor survey (GEM 2014), the "early-stage entrepreneurial activity" rate in France is relatively low (5.3%), even though according to the same source one French person out of three (28.26%) was aware of entrepreneurial opportunities around them. Several reasons are cited for this gap, such as the fear of failure, the economic crisis, a hostile environment, lack of entrepreneurial spirit and competencies. In order to overcome these obstacles, the French Ministry of Higher Education and Research has encouraged universities to develop a kind of "entrepreneurship campaign" aimed at promoting entrepreneurial activities. In recent years, as a result, many programs have been created in business or engineering schools as well as in other domains of higher education (Arlotto *et al.* 2011).

In 2014, the Ministry of Higher Education created 29 entrepreneurship networks all across the French territory. Called PEPITE (a French acronym that means both "seed" or "Pole For Student Innovation, Technology Transfer and Entrepreneurship"), these networks of higher education institutions are supported by the creation of the "entrepreneurial student" status, which extends social security and training benefits for French graduates below the age of 28. This was an important step towards the idea of building "entrepreneurial universities" as evoked by Clark (1998); according to this ideal, universities should have an entrepreneurial-centric culture as the basis for research and teaching, should be administratively more independent and financially more accountable, relying less on public funds. They must thus find a balance between the traditional academic values and a more market-oriented culture (Rinne and Koivula 2005; Shattock 2005). The Bill on Univeristy Liberty and Responsibility, which was voted in 2007 by French lawmakers, is part of the same trend. In this context, to foster entrepreneurship, vocations became one of the ambitions of the French university system in recent years.

<table>
<tr><th>Objectives</th><th>Examples</th><th>French university initiatives</th></tr>
<tr><td rowspan="3">1. Raise awareness</td><td>Meetings with business leaders in various forms (conferences, forums, congresses, etc.)</td><td rowspan="3">Guest lecturers
Vocational service
Apprenticeship service
Junior enterprise (student-run business consulting bureau)</td></tr>
<tr><td>Startup weekend</td></tr>
<tr><td>Organization of competitions</td></tr>
<tr><td>2. Develop competencies</td><td>Entrepreneurial training; Course on new venture creation/SMB acquisition; business games, business model and business plan development tools</td><td>Undergraduate curriculum, continuing education programs</td></tr>
<tr><td>3. Provide support</td><td>Mentoring new venture creation projects
Mentoring SMB acquisition projects</td><td>Pre-incubators, incubators, accelerators, FabLabs, co-working spaces, enterprising student status, e-learning resources (entrepreneurial student degree)</td></tr>
</table>

Table 1.2. *Examples of entrepreneurial initiatives in French universities encouraged by the PEPITE program*

1.3.2. *Enablers of entrepreneurship and innovation education*

Figure 1.6 presents the framework derived from our conceptual and empirical investigation. The three key roles of the university are presented as a triangle (raising awareness, developing skills and providing support). Elements that impact all three dimensions are clustered under the "strategic enablers" tag. Those that have an impact on "awareness" and "skills" were dubbed "pedagogical enablers". Finally, those in the intersection between "skills" and "support" were called "operational enablers".

Foremost among the strategic enablers stands the notion of collaborative or consultative conception and development of entrepreneurship programs. Involving all stakeholders (internal and external) is necessary in order to ensure that the program will reflect a shared vision; at the heart of this consultation process is of course a debate with the students themselves, whose specific needs and expectations must be taken into account in order to better impact their attitudes and behaviors. Based on this diagnosis, a teacher-training program must be designed not only to update instructors on entrepreneurship best practices but also to help them better understand entrepreneurial attitudes and values, as well as project-based pedagogy and active learning resources. This process can be enriched by encouraging teacher engagement in the entrepreneurial ecosystem, visiting incubators and technology parks and exchanging their role with real-life entrepreneurs for one day ("live my life" approach).

Among the operational enablers, formal partnerships between the university and the innovation clusters should help consolidate these learning networks. Furthermore, the university should create at least one physical *locus* to facilitate face-to-face interactions among students and members of the entrepreneurial ecosystem. Ideally, this place should be a multi-purpose environment suitable for informal meetings, coaching sessions and workshops, and animated by weekly activities such as seminars, breakfasts with entrepreneurs and community building programs. It should be decorated in bright colors and mobile furniture, drawing inspiration from Silicon Valley open spaces that are designed to encourage creativity and well-being. It should also incentivize the "FabLab" culture, with prototyping tools such as 3D printers and sketching software. Finally, attention should be paid to the financial mechanisms available. If private investors and angels are not locally available, then the university could create an institutional program to award seed money to the best startups. At the bare minimum, there should be training programs on how to prepare a crowdfunding campaign using platforms such as Kickstarter or Indiegogo.

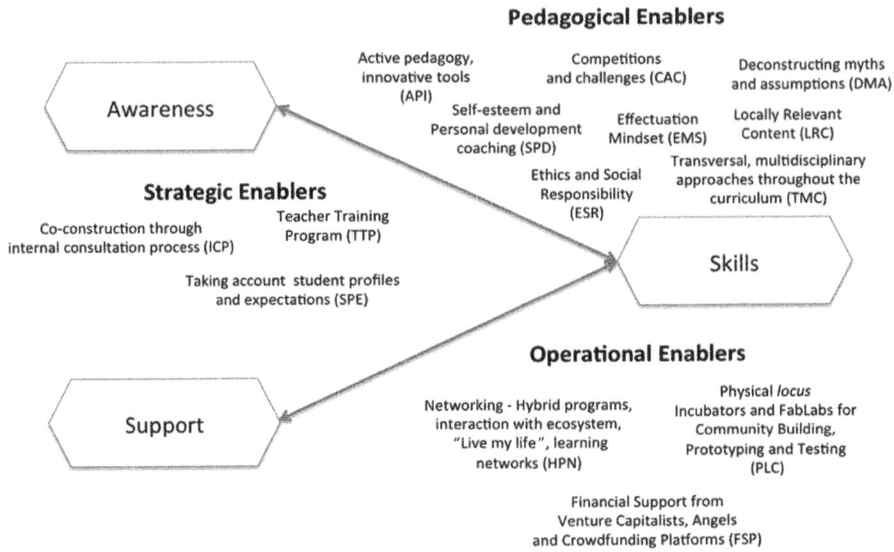

Figure 1.6. *Framework for evaluating effectiveness of entrepreneurship education (Albertini* et al. *2019). For a color version of the figure, see http://www.iste.co.uk/lima/entrepreneurship.zip*

Among the pedagogical enablers, the use of innovative tools based on active learning and real-life projects should be a priority. Rather than having only traditional lectures based on slides, students should also be immersed in simulations, role-playing games, competitions and challenges. Myths and false assumptions about entrepreneurship must be deconstructed; lectures by former students who have created successful local businesses should dispel common misconceptions and demonstrate how any "normal" person can become an entrepreneur. This approach must be reinforced by group dynamics and coaching sessions aimed at developing the sense of self-worth concerning the student's abilities to lead in an innovative environment. Due to the Cartesian training of students, they tend to reason in terms of cause-and-effect patterns that seldom match the complex reality of consumer needs and aspirations. They need therefore to understand the logic of effectuation inherent in principles such as Design Thinking and the Lean Startup approach in order to test their ideas sooner and let the market decide how products and services should be developed. They need to understand their role as "movers and shakers" of societal status quo and the ethical responsibilities that this implies. Finally, all of these initiatives must be transversal and multidisciplinary, involving diverse faculty members who clearly understand their role in creating an entrepreneurial environment throughout the curriculum.

We propose a diagnostic tool in the form of an online questionnaire (Appendix 2). The questionnaire uses a five-point Likert scale to determine the gap between ideal practices and the current perceived reality of Universities (which will be an average of the perceptions of the experts involved and may vary from 1 ("strongly disagree") to 5 ("strongly agree"). Figure 1.7 illustrates the evaluation of the University of Corsica entrepreneurship program by the same experts who participated in the qualitative study.

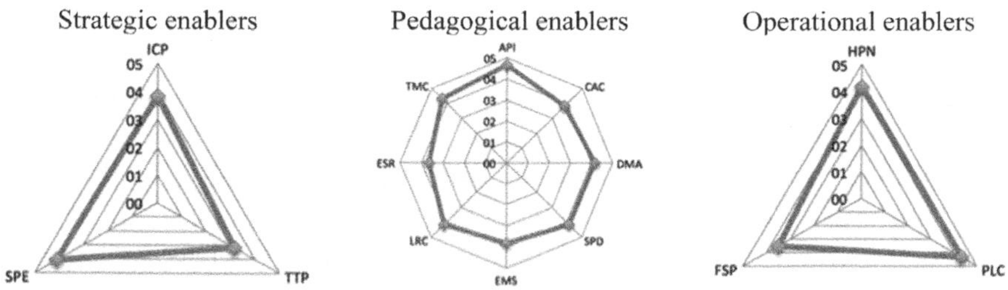

Figure 1.7. *Enablers of the entrepreneurial environment at University of Corsica (Albertini* et al. *2019). For a color version of the figure, see http://www.iste.co.uk/lima/entrepreneurship.zip*

A quantitative analysis of the survey results indicates that Corsica's greatest perceived weakness among the strategic enablers is the teacher training program or TTP (3.2 on the five-point scale). Among the pedagogical enablers, the effectuation mindset (EMS = 3.8) and ethics and social responsibility (ESR = 3.7) are the weakest spots. Among the operational enablers, finance support is the greatest perceived vulnerability (FSP = 3.5). This quick analysis suggests that in order to improve entrepreneurial intent among students, Corsican policy makers should focus their attention on improving teacher education programs that not only emphasize the tools and techniques for creating new ventures but also promote behavioral changes concerning effectuation and risk-taking attitudes. Moreover, these training programs need to underscore the importance of ethical behavior and the potential of social entrepreneurship as an opportunity to improve society. Finally, it seems clear from the data that

Corsica's entrepreneurship environment lacks financial support mechanisms, venture capitalists and angel investors. Attracting those stakeholders or creating state-sponsored programs would likely stimulate students to create new businesses.

1.3.3. *Perspectives for the European ecosystem*

The ultimate output of Pittaway and Cope's framework (2007) is the quantity and quality of interactions in the entrepreneurship and innovation ecosystem, resulting in sustainable economic growth. As discussed in detail in this chapter, the European Commission has identified the right "input" elements in this framework: support E&I education, simplify the legal barriers to create and dissolve startups, strengthen the financial mechanisms that foster entrepreneurial activities and promote a culture of risk taking among first-time entrepreneurs and veteran venture creators, among other measures. According to Carayannis *et al.* (2012), this political/legal capital must be combined with social capital from the civil society. In that sense, media, non-governmental organizations and citizens must be made aware of the value of entrepreneurship and innovation to society. This will increase the social status of entrepreneurs and value-creating individuals, awakening vocations among not only the youth entering the higher education system but also unemployed or inactive people. It will also make current small business owners more aware of the importance of innovation in order to achieve sustainable growth.

Besides political and social capital as inputs, the higher education process must develop adapted programs to create human capital with the right mindset and skills. As seen in this chapter, this involves identifying the ontological specificities of E&I education before asking who, what, how and how-to-evaluate questions, as suggested by Fayolle and Gailly (2008). Concerning the central "how" question, we offer a set of pedagogical, strategic and operational enablers that, taken together, could help raise awareness, develop entrepreneurial hard and soft competencies and provide support to the development of E&I activities by venture-creating students (Albertini *et al.* 2019). One important element that is often forgotten in E&I programs is the fifth dimension of the Carayannis' Quintuple Helix: sustainable development. In order to achieve sustainability (not only ecologically speaking but also in terms of long-term economic development perspectives), it is not only enough to understand the constraints of a fragile ecological environment but also to internalize deep ethical and moral principles that should be associated with the power of value creation.

If all the elements of these nested frameworks are considered, then we believe that the answer to the age-old question "can entrepreneurship be taught" is a resounding YES. Contrary to what Akola and Heinonen (2006) suggest, we have experienced how active learning pedagogy combined with the right academic and business environment and supported by relevant public policies can lead to the development of soft skills such as creativity, innovative thinking, communication and negotiation and leadership. The rest of this book will discuss such pedagogical approaches in depth.

1.4. Collaborative Interactivity learning principles[3]

Most modern educators would agree that students learn very little merely from listening to a teacher or watching his or her slides. According to Spencer (1991), people generally remember only 10% of what they read, 20% of what they hear, 30% of what they see, 50% of what they see and hear, 70% of what they say during a discussion and 90% of what they say while performing actions related to the speech content. This realization has inspired a century-old educational movement originally based on the cognitive development theories of Jean Piaget and Lev Vygotsky (Jonassen *et al.* 1999). Piaget found that humans create meaning by establishing an interaction between their experiences and their ideas. Vygotsky gave birth to the notion of "social constructivism" by emphasizing that learning is inherently a sociocultural process. These founders have inspired the notion of situated cognition, which postulates that knowledge is an inter-subjective construction mediated by social interactions and technological tools in communities of practice.

In my PhD thesis (Lima 2003), I have synthesized these theoretical foundations in a principle I called "Collaborative Interactivity" to express the two fundamental elements of social constructivism (interaction and collaboration). This approach has the following premises: (a) knowledge is mostly self-constructed, which means that it is not entirely transmissible; (b) the construction of knowledge results largely from symbolic action and

3 This section is based on a translation of excerpts from my PhD thesis entitled (in Brazilian Portuguese) "Potential of cognitive support of dynamic hypertextual interfaces" (Lima 2003).

manipulation, so learning is embedded in proactive interaction between the learners and the objects surrounding them (both conceptual and empirical); (c) knowledge is deeply linked to the context in which the action takes place; and (d) meaning is intrinsic to the mind of the knower, not only available externally. Corollaries of this definition are (d1) there are multiple world perspectives; (d2) learning is driven by problem situations of high significance for the learner; (d3) knowledge requires articulation, expression and representation of what is learned; (d4) meaning must be shareable and socially negotiated; and (d5) learning tools can increase the potential for reflection learning (Jonassen *et al.* 1999).

According to these premises, we must satisfy three interdependent conditions for the student to "make sense" of what he or she is learning or "construct" meaning: he or she must have some degree of active control of the learning process (it must be interactive), he or she must be led to articulate concepts around his or her experience (situated reflection) and he or she must be able to discuss his or her insights with others (collaboration). Furthermore, the context of learning must involve authentic, relevant scenarios he or she can clearly identify with. The concept of "Collaborative Interactivity", as illustrated in Figure 1.8, aims at incorporating these three elements: interaction, reflection and collaboration in an authentic learning environment.

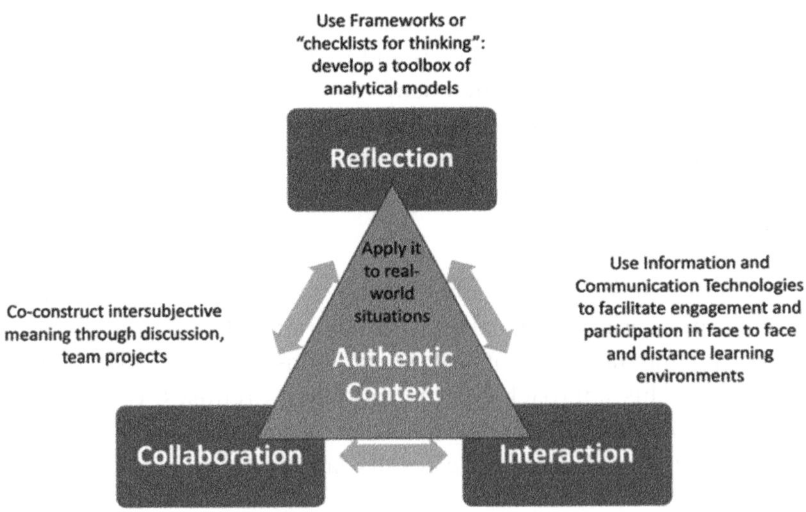

Figure 1.8. *Concept of Collaborative Interactivity (adapted from Lima 2003). For a color version of the figure, see http://www.iste.co.uk/lima/entrepreneurship.zip*

These elements of Collaborative Interactivity are consensually viewed by socio-constructivists as essential to the process of meaningful learning (Jonassen *et al.* 1999). According to this model, individual reflection must be accompanied by *collaboration*, or the inter-subjective negotiation of meaning. Social constructivists believe that group work offers a privileged space for exchanging experiences and creating a better understanding of reality. Lucena and Fuks (2000, p. 109) suggest that collaboration makes it possible to share a wide variety of learning and problem-solving strategies. This happens because collaboration puts individuals in a position to explain and convince others about their own cognitive processes, which facilitates metacognition or "learning about how I think" (Greer *et al.* 2000). According to Berlo (1999), a fundamental aspect of collaboration is the gain of multiple perspectives on the problems addressed. When two people interact, they put themselves in each other's place, trying to perceive the world from each other's perspective. As already discussed, particularly in poorly structured knowledge domains, such as social sciences, using different points of view is an adequate strategy to compose the inter-subjective reality.

The second dimension consists of stimulating the *interaction* between the learner, the learning objects and the facilitator as an effective way to construct knowledge. The expression "learning-*by-doing*" has become commonplace beyond pedagogical circles due to the fact that, as already discussed, much of the knowledge required to do analytical work is tacit, requiring experimentation and socialization to be internalized (Nonaka and Takeushi 1995). Information and communication technologies (ICT) can provide effective ways of interacting with concepts and empirical data. Business simulation games, interactive case studies and distance learning tools are just a few examples of how ICT can make the learning experience more interactive, even when dealing with a large number of participants. Other examples will be given at the end of each chapter.

Collaboration and interaction lead to individual *reflection*. In order to learn from their reflections, students need a certain structure or model of spatial information and establishing relationships between them. In addition to making the experiences more meaningful, Jonassen and his co-authors (1999) suggest that instigating students to systematize their own information in order to produce hypotheses makes them more involved with the resulting knowledge. When they simply receive and reprocess information given by third parties, they are far less committed. For this reason, the main objective of teachers in business schools should be to give students "thinking tools" that help them structure their problem-solving approaches. This book lists dozens of such tools in the form of analytical frameworks or "checklists for thinking".

Unlike interaction, reflection and collaboration, *contextualization* is not an activity but a quality inherent in the Collaborative Interactivity environment, which increases the perceived relevance of the three elements. Research shows that learning done in a context close to the professional reality experienced by the learner results in knowledge that is more easily transferable to new situations (Jonassen *et al.* 1999). Selinger (2001, pp. 96–105) defines as authentic those tasks that lead students to recognize their previous experiences in the learning process. According to this principle, teachers should create problems that lead students to access previous knowledge and apply it as if he or she were acting as a professional (Mãtta 2001). Young (1995) emphasizes 10 essential attributes of "real-world" problems that must be respected in authentic learning contexts:

– the solution of such problems requires the coordination of multiple cognitive processes, such as analysis, planning, problem identification and metacognitive reflection;

– the credibility of the context increases the critical perceptions about viable situations;

– solutions in these contexts tend to be negotiated inter-subjectively, facilitating collaboration;

– technology can play a fundamental role in this process of interpersonal problem solving, facilitating communication and interaction among participants;

– solving complex real-world problems often requires an interdisciplinary approach and should, if possible, involve people with different skills/knowledge/biases;

– such problems often give rise to multiple competing solutions; there are no "correct" answers, but different degrees of viability;

– it is necessary to distinguish between relevant information and little useful information; real problems often bring a lot of superfluous information, and such insight is part of the skills that are expected to develop in professionals working in ill-structured knowledge domains, such as business and social sciences.

The enumeration of these attributes illustrates how a learning environment with authentic situations leads to the convergence of the other components of the Collaborative Interactivity model. Taken in isolation, none of them reach their full potential. When applied together, they create a rich, immersive learning experience that can be particularly effective in the domain of innovation and entrepreneurship education. Throughout this book, each chapter will finish with a few suggestions on how to teach specific E&I tools using the Collaborative Interactivity model.

2

From Idea to Vision[1]

A legendary hero is usually the founder of something – the founder of a new age, the founder of a new religion, the founder of a new city, the founder of a new way of life. In order to found something new, one has to leave the old and go on a quest of the seed idea, a germinal idea that will have the potential of bringing forth that new thing.

Joseph Campbell,
Hero with a Thousand Faces

According to Louis Jacques Filion (1991), the entrepreneur is someone who imagines, develops and fulfills his or her visions. The vision is an idea, or a set of ideas and goals (images) that one wishes to achieve in the future. He presents three categories of visions: the emergent vision (primary), the central vision and the complementary vision (see Figure 2.1).

The emergent visions result from ideas about products and/or services imagined by the entrepreneur before he or she starts a new venture. At this stage, the entrepreneur has but a very foggy image of what the final enterprise features will be. He or she is usually "inspired" by a sudden insight as to what the product should be like, what makes it unique and which market needs it is supposed to fulfill, not knowing yet whether the

1 A few excerpts from this chapter were previously published as an article by Lima and Dolabela (2000).

idea is economically feasible or where to find the financial resources to develop it.

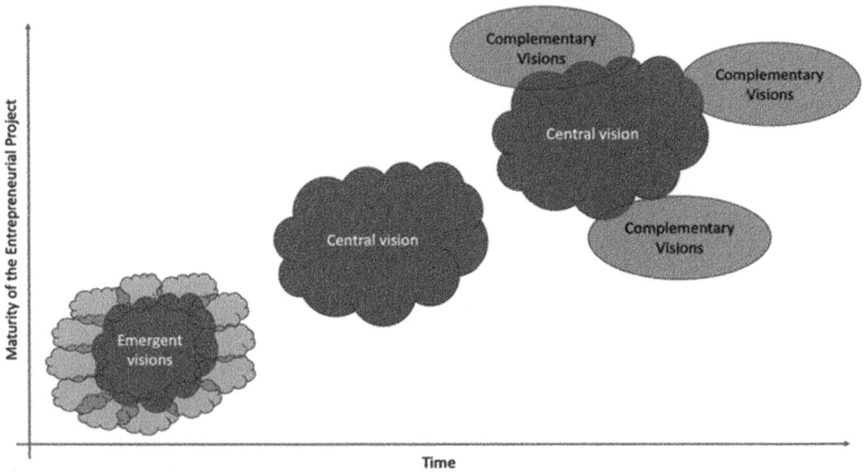

Figure 2.1. *Progression from emergent to central to complementary visions (based on Filion 1991). For a color version of the figure, see http://www.iste.co.uk/lima/entrepreneurship.zip*

The central vision is a result from one single emergent vision or from a combination of emergent visions. The entrepreneur has at this point spent enough time preparing a business plan or business model or even carrying out the economic activity to know well some of the actual cost factors, market potential, strengths, weaknesses, opportunities and threats involved. At this stage, the idea has evolved into a clearly defined scope of action. The initial production or service delivery capacity has been set, the sources of financial support have been negotiated and the prototypes and pre-launch operations have been fully tested and approved.

Complementary visions are related to managerial aspects of the new venture supporting the central vision. Some of these "operational advancements" include logistics improvements, learn-by-doing innovations, product enhancements, market segmentation and adjustment of the enterprise structure to optimum performance.

According to the results presented by Filion's research, many entrepreneurs are unsuccessful because they fail to distinguish between a business idea and a business opportunity. Many emergent visions have led the wrong persons to undertake the wrong business at the wrong time. An opportunity is a business idea in the hands of someone capable of identifying the resources to successfully implement it and make it grow. Accordingly, entrepreneurial visions are likely to be successfully fulfilled depending on five basic factors:

a) The amount of self-knowledge and maturity for the new undertaking ("Am I the right person to fulfill this unmet need?").

b) Their leadership capacity.

c) The personal energy they are willing and able to put into their project.

d) The knowledge the entrepreneur can acquire on the product or service he/she is developing and its market.

e) The relationship network they can build.

Knowledge of the self and knowledge of the business seem to be the most important supporting factor to any visionary process. Figure 2.2 illustrates the relationship between each of these concepts.

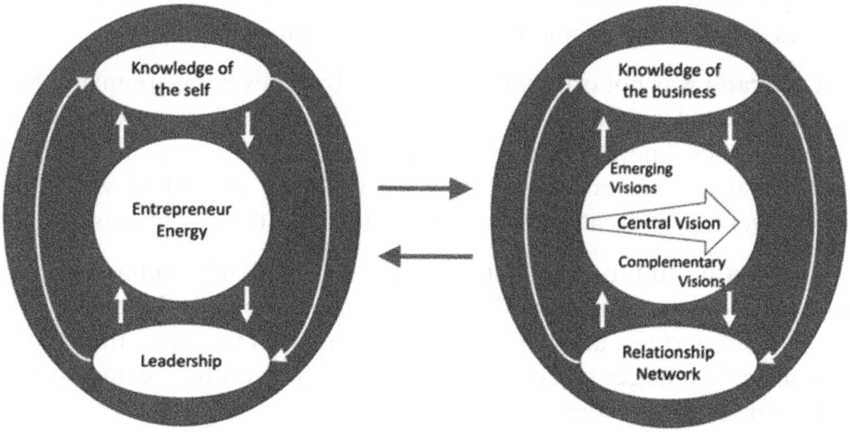

Figure 2.2. *Relationship between elements supporting the entrepreneur's visionary process (adapted from Filion 1991). For a color version of the figure, see http://www.iste.co.uk/lima/entrepreneurship.zip*

2.1. Self-knowledge: follow thy passion

One of the most important pieces of advice an E&I teacher can give a student is to prioritize projects in a business domain you already know well. In the case of students, this is often the case in the domains for which they have a personal involvement out of a childhood passion. An individual's self-image will directly influence what he or she can accomplish as an entrepreneur. An important part of the entrepreneurship methodology based on Filion's theory consists precisely of making students aware that the enterprises they create will necessarily be an extension of what they are as human beings. We project the future based on what we are and how we view the world. Therefore, it is necessary to know oneself in order to know what kind of business one can create and operate. As an entrepreneur, one must constantly ask oneself what he or she finds appealing in a specific business area and how they can do that better or different than others.

One innovation concept that can help students understand this dimension is Eric Von Hippel's notion of "lead users" (Von Hippel 1988). As illustrated by Figure 2.3, lead users feel an urge to create a solution to a problem even before such a solution is commercially available. They are passionate experts who are not necessarily interested in creating a business out of their solution, but they do understand the unmet need so deeply that they often tinker a solution to their own problem. The following are examples of historically famous lead user innovations:

– **Gatorade** was not originally developed by a beverage company, but by athletes who understood the need to replenish more than water after their exertions – they knew that during their exercises they also lost salts and minerals that are not contained in water from tap or bottled water. They therefore went on to create such a liquid, adding all those elements.

– **Mountain biking** was not invented by a biking company, but by passionate cyclists who needed a lighter, more versatile bike that would allow them to perform acrobatics and face tough terrain. They tinkered with lighter materials, larger wheels and better designs until they came up with a prototype that would address their needs.

– **The World Wide Web** was originally created by Sir Tim Berners-Lee at CERN as a solution to his own need to share documents in hypertext format. He programmed a protocol to facilitate these networked exchanges (now known by the acronym HTTP – Hypertext Transfer Protocol) and a language to create these documents (HTML – HyperText Markup Language). Thus, the modern ubiquitous Internet interface was not designed by IBM, Microsoft or Apple, but by a community of enthusiasts who embraced Sir Tim's open source code.

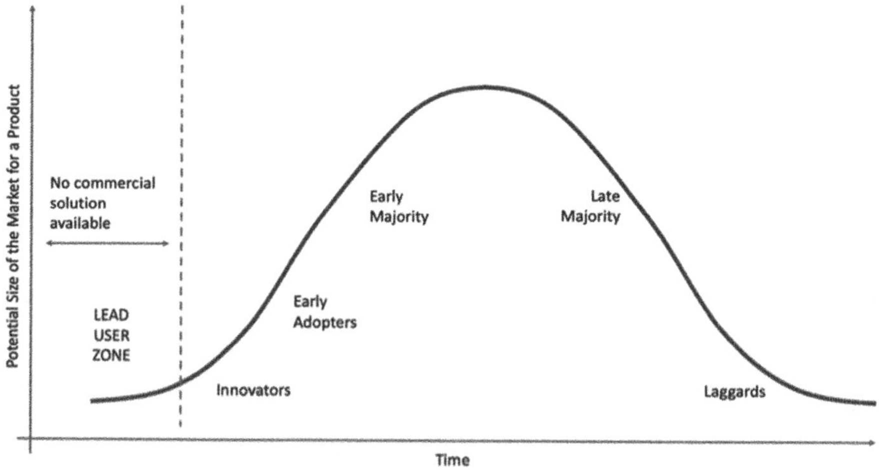

Figure 2.3. *Lead users develop a solution to a deeply felt need before it is commercially available (adapted from Von Hippel, 1988). For a color version of the figure, see http://www.iste.co.uk/lima/entrepreneurship.zip*

Even if the entrepreneurs-to-be are not necessarily part of the lead user community, the fact that they share a passion with this community will make it easier for them to exploit their weak ties to that community, facilitating the exploration of unmet needs not yet exploited by competing solutions.

2.2. Knowledge of the business field

Filion (1991) detected that the ability to find a business opportunity and develop a vision is correlated with the knowledge of the business field involved. Knowing the business field means understanding the way competing enterprises are organized in the sector, what some of the negotiation procedures are, who the customers are how they behave and what their buying potential is, what the critical success factors in this business are and how to increase the competitive advantage of the enterprise. Entrepreneurs must understand the technology involved, short- and medium-term market expectations, legal aspects of the business, the supply chain and the profile of the people they will have to hire. Many interviews with entrepreneurs reveal that "intuition" rather than "knowledge" was a key factor contributing to the success of the business. Thus, an entrepreneur's intuition capacity is directly related to the amount of time spent getting to know a specific business area.

Several E&I frameworks and tools are available to help students deepen their knowledge of the business environment (see a detailed discussion in the next chapter):

– PESTEL analysis – a checklist to help students think about most dimensions of the external environment of any business. It facilitates the categorization of opportunities and threats in the political, economic, socio-cultural, technological, ecological and legal spheres.

– Porter's Five Forces – a classic tool created by Harvard Professor Michel Porter for identifying competitive threats from newcomers, existing rivals, substitutes, suppliers and customers, helping identify potential entry barriers (or lack thereof).

– Porter's Value Chain – another tool created by Porter to identify strengths and weaknesses in secondary activities (human, financial, material and informational resource management) and primary activities (logistics, operations, marketing and after-sales).

– Market STP (Segmentation, Targeting and Positioning) – marketing framework to identify strengths and weaknesses associated with the choice of segments and brand positioning.

– Marketing 4Ps – strengths and weaknesses inherent in product, place, promotion and pricing decisions based on the choices of targeting and positioning.

– TOWS matrix – a sophisticated tool to create offensive and defensive strategies based on the most relevant opportunities/threats coupled with strengths and weaknesses identified with the frameworks above.

We will discuss these tools in more detail in Chapter 3 ("From Vision to Business Plan"). The most important insight for teachers and students here is to realize that the data for these analyses should be obtained from credible sources and databases. Most business schools have access to one or several of the following databases (in alphabetical order):

– Business Source Ultimate (BSU) – academic articles, market analyses, company profiles, country profiles

– Dalloz – law and jurisprudence

– EconBiz – academic literature, business studies and economic trends

– Emerald database – academic articles

– Factiva – press articles, international trends, trade articles, company data

– Freedom Collection (Science Direct) – academic articles

– JSTOR database – academic articles

– Navis Fiscal – legal trends, jurisprudence

– Orbis – company + financial data, financial analyses

– ProQuest database – academic articles, company data, financial and banking data

– Scholarvox by Cyberlibris – e-books, virtual textbooks

– SciVal database – academic articles, bibliometric studies

– Scopus database – academic articles, bibliometric studies

– Xerfi Knowledge – market studies, industry analyses, company analyses, economic news

Appendix 3 presents a comprehensive list of commonly used databases in business schools. They should be used as sources of secondary data for the analysis of business environments.

2.3. Relationship networks

Among all elements supporting the entrepreneurial vision, the relationship network is considered one of the most important ones. Filion's research has found that the inner family circle, what he calls the "primary relationships", is the main motivating environment for entrepreneurs. Most successful entrepreneurs interviewed during his research displayed some kind of family or childhood context that led to their entrepreneurial decision. Family continues to be the primary source of advice concerning the further development of the entrepreneurial vision throughout the entrepreneur's cycle. The "secondary relationships" are also very significant. Close friends, members of a club or society, suppliers and regular customers are all important contributors to the entrepreneur's vision. Finally, the "tertiary relationships" are not only other people but also books, specialized magazines, trips and congresses that lead to what Mark Granovetter famously called "weak ties".

In 1973, Granovetter published what would become one of the most cited papers of all time in social sciences (over 55,000 citations on Google Scholar as of March 2020). Called "The Strength of Weak Ties", this article argued that social opportunities are more easily detectable through one's secondary social network connections (so-called "weak ties") than through one's closest relations (family, friends and colleagues). Granovetter (1973, p. 1361) defines the strength of an interpersonal tie as the "combination of the amount of time, the emotional intensity, the intimacy (mutual confiding), and the reciprocal services which characterize the tie". His breakthrough insight consisted of hypothesizing that people outside your immediate social sphere are not only more numerous, but much more diverse and thus more likely to be familiar with diverse social opportunities, such as job openings, inside information or overall market trends.

Such insight would prove premonitory of the role of social networks in the 21st Century. Indeed, tools such as LinkedIn, Twitter or Facebook provide nowadays millions of weak ties, allowing modern entrepreneurs to monitor opportunities and threats by crowdsourcing their list of online contacts. Thus, if relationship networks were important 30 years ago, when Filion proposed his visionary theory, it has become even more so in the age of social networks.

In Filion's model depicted in Figure 2.2, it is interesting to note how relationship networks feed both the vision and knowledge of the business while also being fed by them. Indeed, the more one gets in contact with potential customers, competitors, suppliers, government agencies and university experts, the more one develops the vision from the emerging to the central and complementary stages. At the same time, these interactions help develop a better understanding of the business, its industry and market opportunities and threats.

The implications of this trend for E&I education are evident: one must include social networking and community management skills in any modern entrepreneurship and innovation curriculum. Students must understand how to develop their personal network, how to create a personal brand and cultivate online contacts. They must realize the importance of "crowdsourcing" information by soliciting opinions, ideas and facts to their "online followers". They must play with social media management tools (such as HootSuite, Khoros, Lumly and Sprout Social), which allow them to create a visual dashboard to monitor trends on widespread networks such as Twitter, Facebook, Instagram, LinkedIn, YouTube and Reddit.

2.4. Other factors contributing to the development of the vision

Leadership and personal energy are the two other critical factors presented by Filion's model. Their importance to the success of an enterprise is very easily perceived: without the ability to influence people and to motivate them, "contaminating" them with his or her ideas, an entrepreneur certainly will not make much progress. Leadership is thus a common element found in all successful entrepreneurs. However, if an entrepreneur is not capable of dedicating a lot of his or her personal time and concentration to developing the vision, it will very unlikely come true. Entrepreneurs are known for the amount of personal energy they put into their ideas; even when they have to work at night and during weekends while holding a job during the week, entrepreneurs must be in love with what they are about to create if it is to be successful. Students being prepared to start their own businesses according to this methodology are always made aware that being one's own boss usually means sacrificing a lot of one's spare time and family contact.

The ideas discussed above have been the main theoretical background for entrepreneurship learning in many institutions of higher education across the globe. Using Filion's methodology, students have been prepared to release their creative energy and identify business opportunities regardless of the study field they are engaged in. Such methodology includes topics on how to develop visions and build relationship networks, what the typical entrepreneurial profile is, how to promote creative thinking, identifying and exploiting business opportunities, writing a business plan and interviewing successful entrepreneurs as a reference. Sharing case studies about passionate people who solved widespread problems could be a source of motivation to inspire future entrepreneurs.

It is important to note the interdependent nature of all the elements in Filion's model. As we previously saw, increasing one's relationship networks leads to better knowledge of the business environment and nurtures the vision. Likewise, a better understanding of one's own passions and abilities is crucial to understand in which domain one has the potential to become a leader innovator. There is a virtuous cycle intrinsic in finding out one's true passion: being knowledgeable and passionate about that domain will naturally lead entrepreneurs to increase their relationship network and their knowledge of that sector, increasing the entrepreneurial energy necessary to start the new venture.

As we will see in Chapter 5 when we discuss Design Thinking, an important aspect of choosing one's own passion as a cornerstone of one's entrepreneurial project is one's ability to develop empathy. It is easier to "feel the pain" of customers if this is a domain in which the innovators themselves deeply experience an unmet need.

2.5. Teaching the visionary theory

We will finish every chapter in this book with a few suggestions on how to apply the principles of Collaborative Interactivity to the topic in question. This will involve discussing ways to make teaching the topic more authentic by applying project-based pedagogical approaches, which are more interactive and collaborative through the use of technology and more reflective through prescribing individual exercises for conceptual application.

2.5.1. *Reflecting about the visionary model*

The ideal way to present the visionary framework is through storytelling. Videos about passionate individuals who achieved their visions as lead users are a valuable resource. Famous examples include how Phil Knight developed his vision for Nike, how Steve Jobs envisioned computers for ordinary people at Apple and how Jeff Bezos dreamed of the "everything store". As inspirational as these well-known hero journeys may be, they can also be intimidating. Students may think, "I'm not like Steve Jobs", and simply decide that entrepreneurship is the domain of geniuses. To counterbalance this trend, it is also useful to invite small business founders to give testimonials. One can also show short clips of interviews with alumni and their own stories of success and failure in their entrepreneurship adventure. It may be quite useful to introduce the concept of lead-user innovation. Eric von Hippel has a number of interesting videos about this concept on YouTube, and his book "The Sources of Innovation" is freely available for download. It could also be useful to present Grenovetter's theory about the strength of weak ties and the role of social media (particularly LinkedIn) in expanding one's relationship network.

This is a good place to promote a debate about "nature versus nurture" in entrepreneurship. Can anyone become an entrepreneur? It is important to use the elements in the model to emphasize that, even if talent helps, most of the competences in entrepreneurship can be acquired. This is the case with knowledge of the business, network development and leadership skills.

2.5.2. *Creating an authentic context*

Each student should be required to work on their own individual vision, whether they intend to start a new business in the next few months, years or decades. They will all be at the "emergent vision" stage initially. In a short entrepreneurship course (just a few hours), it is unlikely that many students will move to the central vision and complementary vision stages. This is perfectly normal; it takes time and reflection to develop a mature vision. If the emergent vision is well anchored in the learner's mind during this initiation, it will stick with them long after the course is over and will gradually mature over time.

2.5.3. *Making it more interactive*

A good way to guide students through the visionary process is to create an online self-diagnosis questionnaire using tools such as Google Forms (https://docs.google.com/forms/) or Microsoft Forms (https://forms.office.com/). Questions should be asked in an intuitive way to help students think through the framework, for instance:

– Knowledge of the self/energy/leadership: What are you passionate about? Why are you passionate about this topic? If you didn't have any other constraints, how many hours a week would you be willing to work on developing a product or service in this domain? What kind of people would you hire to help you if you had the resources?

– Emerging vision: Can you think of an unmet need in your domain of passion? Can you think of a product or service to address that need?

– Knowledge of the business/network: How would you grade yourself on a scale of knowledge about this industry? (0 = ignorant, 5 = expert). How can you learn more about it? List all the people you know who are directly or indirectly involved in this industry. How can you expand this list?

The beauty of using an online form platform for inputting individual data is that it is quite easy to extract a spreadsheet with inputs from all the students in the class and share it back with the group (using again Google Drive or Microsoft OneDrive).

2.5.4. *Collaborating*

Once students have had time to prepare their forms, and now that their inputs are visible to everyone in the shared online sheet, it is time to discuss and co-construct. Students can be grouped in threes or fours (using adjacent columns in the shared sheet as a criterion, for instance). In each group, students can take turns presenting their vision and discussing it with others. Those listening to the presenter can assume the roles of consultants, asking "devil's advocate" questions, making comments and contributing ideas. This will allow students to realize how varied the visions can be and to discover unsuspected passions in their comrades. Furthermore, they will share best practices about how to develop their knowledge of the business and their relationship network. If there is enough time, volunteers in each group can make a summary of the discussion to the whole class.

3

From Vision to Business Plan

I keep six honest serving-men
(They taught me all I knew)
Their names are What and Why and When
And How and Where and Who.

Rudyard Kipling,
The Elephant's Child

There is a plethora of business plan templates available for download on the Internet. Most of them have in common the fact that they involve a description of market trends, organizational structure and financial objectives, usually in that order. The structure below is the one we use with our entrepreneurship students.

The first part of a business plan is the executive summary, which is meant to be read by stakeholders in just a few minutes to give them an overview of the plan and convince them to read it fully. It is followed by a contextualization of the idea and the vision, how they evolved and why the proponents of the business plan are the right people to exploit and explore them. Some schools require students to create a literature review after the context, to make sure they know how to research the key concepts surrounding this business domain and industry.

With or without a literature review, every business plan should contain a market analysis, which consists of identifying opportunities and threats in the external environment, then defining a segmentation, targeting and positioning strategy based on these external factors beyond the control of the entrepreneur.

Once the positioning and target are clearly defined (and only then), entrepreneurs can adapt their marketing plan accordingly by developing the product and service mix. With the product and service portfolio clearly defined, it becomes apparent which organizational strategy, structure and systems will be required to deliver them. Porter's Value Chain framework can be used to identify internal strengths and weaknesses.

In the final and arguably most important part of the business plan, students are expected to confront the external trends they do not control (opportunities and threats) with the internal strengths and weaknesses in a TOWS matrix – an advanced SWOT analysis that leads to offensive and defensive strategies. Once an action plan is derived from these strategies, the business plan writer has enough elements to forecast financial objectives and cash flow expectations. This should be done using widely available spreadsheet templates, which make it easy to forecast pessimistic, conservative and optimistic scenarios.

In this final section, a Gantt chart can help visualize all the action plans, with their milestones, bottlenecks and resource allocation challenges. In the appendices, entrepreneurs should list diagrams, pictures and exhibits that would have encumbered the main text. Finally, the plan should be wrapped up with a list of all the secondary sources and bibliographic references used in the literature review and market research process. Each of these steps are described in the sections below.

3.1. Executive summary

The executive summary is to a business plan what an abstract is to an academic article. As its name suggests, this is a synthesis of the whole business plan, intended to be read by potential investors or stakeholders. An executive summary should not take more than two or three pages. Some templates suggest that the main function of the summary is to disseminate a synthetic version of the plan without giving away too many details for the sake of confidentiality. Experienced entrepreneurs know, however, that the potential value of an idea is not necessarily embedded in the way it is planned, but in the actual manner of its execution (see the discussion about business models, below). Inexperienced entrepreneurs tend to often exaggerate the importance of keeping their ideas confidential, and thus fail to receive valuable feedback from potential customers, partners and stakeholders. The executive summary is a good compromise between the two extremes.

The executive summary should contain, at least:

– a brief description of the business opportunity – the main vision, the unmet need;

– a synthesis of the market environment analysis – the main opportunities and threats surrounding the business idea;

– a synthesis of the strategic marketing plan – chosen target and positioning;

– a brief description of the operational marketing plan – the 4Ps (product) or 7Ps (service);

– a short description of the company structure, culture and staff;

– a summary of the expected financial results in a pessimist, conservative and optimistic scenario.

A good executive summary should cover most of the famous 5W+2H questions alluded to in Kipling's poem cited above: what the unmet need is, why you are the right person to address it, how you intend to allocate marketing, organizational and financial resources, a timeline of expected milestones in the short and medium terms, a geographic coverage of your operations, expected costs, break-even point and return over investment.

3.2. Context: vision development

Most investors and future partners care less about the idea than they do about the founders themselves. They know that the idea will evolve and change as the vision develops and the business model is adapted. The founders, however, will stay the same. This section is an important opportunity of answering the question "why we are well positioned to exploit this opportunity?" Entrepreneurs could use Filion's visionary framework discussed in Chapter 2 to discuss the following:

– How did the opportunity evolve from an idea to full-fledged vision?

– Why are you well prepared to take advantage of this opportunity? What makes you well suited to "understand the unmet need"?

– How can your existing relationship network benefit the business development process? How do you intend to expand this network?

– What do you know about the industry/segment? How do you intend to learn more about them?

3.3. Literature review

Some business schools require students to add a literature review at the beginning of their business plans. This should give students the opportunity to familiarize themselves with core academic concepts that could help them better understand the opportunity at hand.

A good way to structure the literature review is to follow the "funnel" principle, as illustrated in Figure 3.1. It holds the premise that the reader of the business plan is not necessarily familiar with the knowledge domain that most directly impacts the project, for instance, "consumer behavior" or "digital marketing". Nor are the readers necessarily familiar with key concepts in those domains. For example, in the digital marketing domain, you may have concepts like search engine optimization or user experience design or sharing economy platforms. Finally, the literature review must describe the industry chosen for the project development, such as the luxury industry or the hospitality industry. By applying the main domain concept to the industry or segment, we obtain a very focused literature review topic.

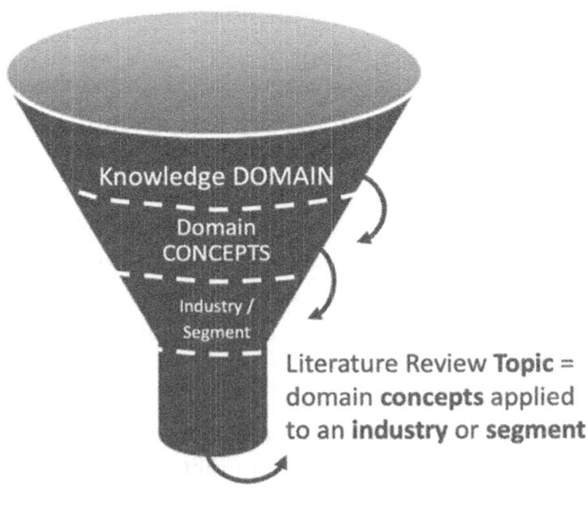

Figure 3.1. *Elements of a funnel-like literature review structure (developed by the author). For a color version of the figure, see http://www.iste.co.uk/lima/entrepreneurship.zip*

From the examples above, we could derive the following literature review topic: “User Experience Design in the Hospitality Industry”. This would be an appropriate project for students in the knowledge domain of digital marketing whose project would be to establish a consulting agency to help independent hotels to improve their e-commerce solutions, for instance. Three levels of literature review would be prepared:

– **Domain level**: the students could start by describing an overview of the DM field (history, main branches, applications, controversies in this field, how consumer experiences have become more convenient in the age of instant gratification, etc.).

– **Concept level**: they could then move on to the concept of UX design and describe, for instance, the role of tools such as Customer Journey Maps in identifying pain points that can be minimized through the development of better interfaces. They can argue about the importance of search engine optimization to remain competitive and the omnichannel solutions to online booking (through affiliation links, intermediary platforms or through autonomous search engine advertising efforts).

– **Industry/segment level**: finally, they can describe the hospitality industry nationally and regionally; the key players and key figures (size of the industry, and how better UX design can help improve the online experience of guests and attract more direct bookings through their own digital assets). They can also briefly describe their targeted segment (independent hotel chains), even though this will be done in more detail in section 3.4.

In order to do this literature review appropriately, students need to have access to databases containing expert articles on the three levels. For the domain and concept levels, academic articles are the best sources. Besides the secondary data sources listed in Appendix 3, students can also make use of Google Scholar. GS has the advantage of giving free access to millions of article journals from all platforms, as it lists the PDFs made available by authors on academic sites such as https://www.researchgate.net/ and https://www.academia.edu/. Another benefit of GS is the fact that it gives the number of citations of each article, helping students to determine their relevance. Finally, GS also allows students to easily import citations in any of the classic referencing standards (MLA, APA, Chicago, Harvard and Vancouver). For the industry/segment analysis, they can use market analysis and industry analysis sources such as Factiva and Xerfi.

A credible literature review will take between 10 and 15 pages and should not only prove that students have become familiar with key concepts in the knowledge domain of their specialization but also give them key insights about trends, opportunities and threats in the external environment.

3.4. Market analysis

This is one of the main parts of any business plan. If the literature review proves that students are familiar with relevant academic concepts and key industry facts, the market analysis shows student expertise in the macro-, meso- and micro-environments of their target market. Figure 3.2 illustrates the several layers of a market analysis.

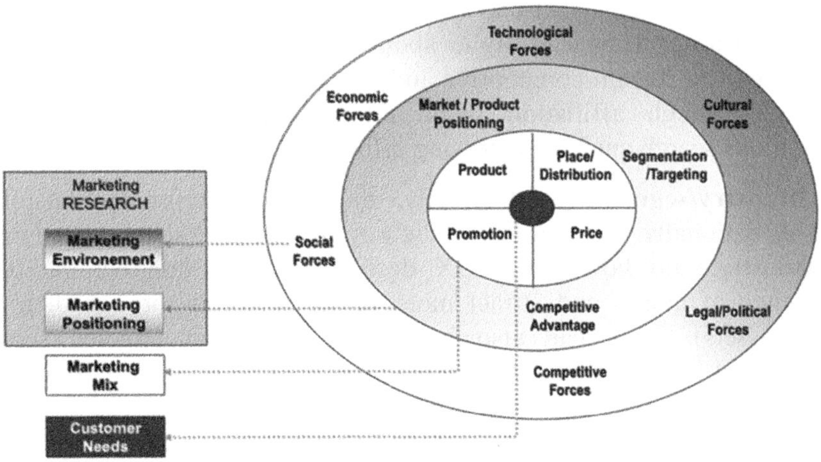

Figure 3.2. *Market analysis: from the marketing environment to the marketing mix. For a color version of the figure, see http://www.iste.co.uk/lima/entrepreneurship.zip*

In this section, students should start with the variables that are beyond their control: opportunities and threats in the political, economic, socio-cultural, technological, ecological and legal environments, as well as those positive and negative trends emerging from the competitive environment.

3.4.1. *Opportunities and threats in the macro-environment: PESTEL-C*

Most business school students are familiar with frameworks for this environment analysis. Known variably as PESTEL or STEEPLE, this popular model is a checklist for researching opportunities and threats, as presented in Figure 3.3.

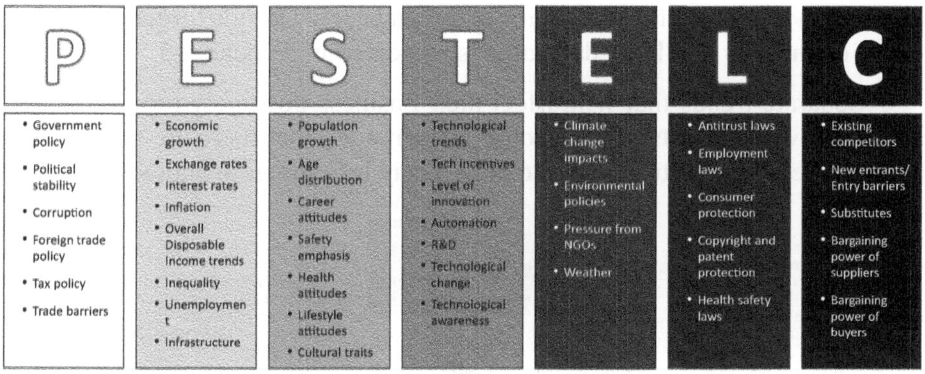

Figure 3.3. *The Political, Economic, Socio-Cultural, Technological, Environmental, Legal and Competitive external environment framework. For a color version of the figure, see http://www.iste.co.uk/lima/entrepreneurship.zip*

Traditional PESTEL analysis often fails to include the "competitor" environment. The seventh column in the above model incorporates the very important sources of competitive advantage (or disadvantage) enumerated by Michael Porter (1980) in his extended rivalry framework (also known as the Five Forces). Figure 3.4 illustrates this model as a separate checklist, allowing students to visualize the role of the five other forces that may threaten new venture development.

Another way to identify opportunities and threats in the competitive environment consists of listing the strengths and weaknesses of direct competitors or substitutes. Their strengths are threats to the entrepreneur, while their weaknesses are opportunities.

These two frameworks combined should give students an extensive "checklist for thinking" about the external environment. Students should be encouraged to adopt the following best practices when contextualizing their PESTEL-C analysis:

– Do some research: students tend to simply brainstorm trends from the top of their heads, which often results in obvious, useless trends (which are frequently unproven). They should be encouraged to use trend databases to identify the most important forces that might affect their business in each dimension. As previously mentioned, business schools often offer free access to very powerful secondary data databases. Do not forget that a full list of commonly available databases is presented in Appendix 3.

– Separate trends that will affect their business positively (opportunities) and negatively (threats): they should be reminded that there are no absolute values here: an opportunity to one player may be a threat to another.

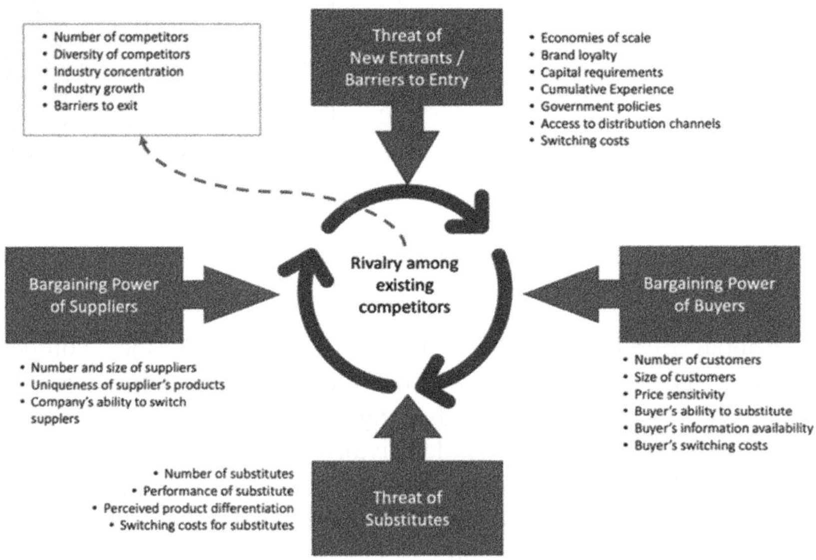

Figure 3.4. *Porter's extended rivalry model (1980). For a color version of the figure, see http://www.iste.co.uk/lima/entrepreneurship.zip*

– Refer to their opportunities and threats using shortcuts O_1, O_2, O_3... O_n; T_1, T_2, T_3... T_n. The space available in the above diagram is too narrow for students to expand on their findings. They can use a visual synthesis with shortcuts and keywords for the sake of brevity, but it should be followed by a paragraph commenting on the most important Os and Ts.

– List only the most relevant opportunities and threats: for the sake of completion, students often list the first trends they find, whether it will affect their business or not. Only highly relevant Os and Ts should be listed, even if some categories are left empty. It is better to focus on the few trends that matter than to disperse their attention with too many irrelevant trends.

3.4.2. *Meso-environment: STP framework*

Whereas the PESTEL-C framework lists elements beyond the control of new venture creators, the meso-environment should be defined based on how the entrepreneur adapts his or her strategy to those opportunities and threats. Figure 3.5 illustrates the key decisions in this process.

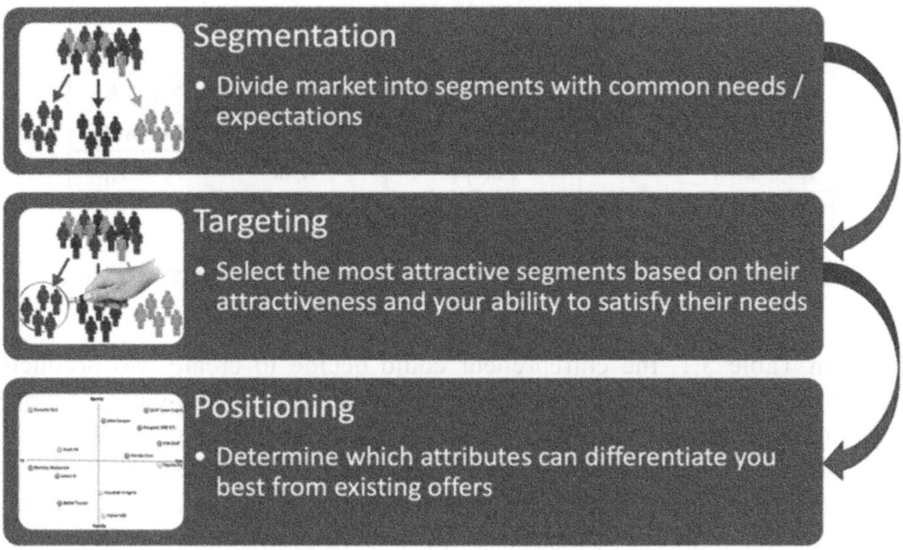

Figure 3.5. *Segmentation–targeting–positioning process. For a color version of the figure, see http://www.iste.co.uk/lima/entrepreneurship.zip*

The first step in this process is to understand all the available segments that the entrepreneur can reach with his or her new venture. Students often make the mistake of jumping too quickly to the profile of the target audience without first considering the alternatives. Let us imagine that a student wishes to create an online travel agency for exotic destinations. Table 3.1 summarizes some of their choices of segments to target.

Note that the first segmentation criterion is probably the most important: do they want to specialize in holiday travels, honeymoon destinations or business tourism? If they choose, for instance, honeymooners, some research into their buying behavior will indicate that it is often the bride who decides about the destination, so the choice of gender for the core target should probably be women. Next, depending on the yearly income level, this agency will specialize in budget, premium or luxury honeymoon packages. They also have to make decisions about the "spirit" of the honeymoon (adventurous, classic, romantic) and where they will focus their partnership network of service providers (Europe, Asia or Americas).

Segmentation criteria	Segment 1	Segment 2	Segment 3
Occasion	**Holidays**	Honeymoon	Business
Age	25–30	**30–40**	>40
Gender	Male	Female	**Both**
Yearly income	> 40 K€ < 80 K€	>80 € < 120 K€	**> 120 K€**
Lifestyle	Adventurous	Classic	**Romantic**
Destination	Europe	**Asia**	Americas
Others			

Table 3.1. *Segmentation table with typical consumer segmentation criteria*

From Table 3.1, the entrepreneur could decide to create two products: adventurous honeymoon packages for young, middle-class couples (highlighted as dark background cells) or holiday trips for married couples looking for a romantic getaway (highlighted with bold fonts). They choose to specialize in Asian destination for both products. They can now create a "persona" (a fictitious character with a biography that translates their characteristics) for each of these targeted segments. Here are two examples:

– **Target 1: Adventurous European honeymooner**. Elisabeth is 29 years old. She is planning her wedding for next summer. She lives in Paris, works at a consulting company at La Défense and is going to attend the *Salon du Mariage*. She follows Instagram accounts about marriage destinations and adrenaline sports. She dreams of a wild, adventurous honeymoon with plenty of thrills and jungle exploration activities in Thailand.

– **Target 2: Exotic anniversary couple**. Steve and Janet are 45 years old. They are both lawyers living in London's Westminster neighborhood. They watch YouTube channels about wildlife, nature and ecology. They also subscribe to podcasts about geopolitics and intercultural differences. Their combined yearly revenue is beyond €120,000 a year, so they expect an exclusive and luxurious experience. They have been married for 10 years and are looking to celebrate this event with a trip to Cambodia's Angkor ruins.

Note how the targets are similar enough to create a synergy in terms of locating suppliers in a geographically restricted area while at the same time having distinct needs and demographic profiles which requires adjusting the operational marketing decisions slightly.

Students must be very careful when choosing their targets, as they must make sure that the chosen segments are

– **attractive**: there are a large enough number of potential customers in the market to make this a profitable business;

– **reachable**: they must understand the target's media and social media habits in order to address specific messages in relevant channels;

– **underserved**: if there are already many competitors with similar products, then this may not be a true opportunity for a competitive new business proposition.

Students often fall into the trap of trying to cover too many different segments, with little synergy between them. They must be reminded that they have limited resources for promotion and product development; therefore, they should keep focused on the most attractive segments (often only one segment initially).

Finally, if they do decide they can outcompete incumbents in this segment, students must choose two or three attributes that will differentiate them from the competitors. This is called "positioning" and is best achieved through a perception map such as the one illustrated by Figure 3.6. A perception map is a visual tool consisting of two axes determining one to four quadrants. Each axis must be labeled with the product attributes that targeted customers perceive as the most valuable (price, quality, design, etc.). A strategic positioning is achieved when a brand occupies a distinctive place in either axis (or preferably both), as compared to competing brands in the same segment, so as to maximize the distance (competitive differentiation) between their brands and the competing offers.

Once the target and positioning of the brand is well established, the entrepreneurs are ready to design their *branding strategy*. The focal point of this strategy will be the creation of a company logo that captures the main attributes of the positioning and clearly appeals to the target. Students can choose between using a freemium tool (such as https://www.canva.com/) to develop their logo and visual identity or hiring the services of a semi-professional designer (an industrial design student, for instance). A slogan is optional but is often a good shortcut to the new company's positioning, vision and values.

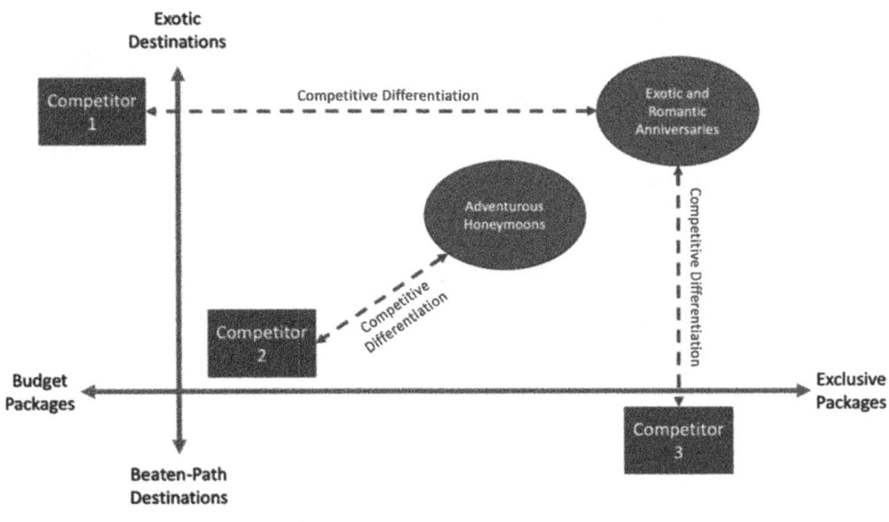

Figure 3.6. *Example of perceptual map for the segmentation table above. For a color version of the figure, see http://www.iste.co.uk/lima/entrepreneurship.zip*

3.5. Marketing plan

In the above section, we covered how to focus the scarce resources of a new venture on the unmet needs of a uniquely defined target with a clearly defined value proposition. Once these have been addressed, the entrepreneur is ready to make decisions about product, pricing, promotion and distribution channels in the operational marketing section. They must constantly keep track of their positioning and targeting while making these 4P decisions and adapt them accordingly.

Figure 3.7 presents a checklist of decisions to be made about the 4Ps of product marketing and the 3Ps of service marketing. The following are examples of questions that new venture creators must answer at this stage of their business plan for product marketing. Each question must be answered based on the *attributes* of the positioning map and target expectations (in our previous example, the need for exclusive and exotic travel experiences by young couples).

– **Product**: How should we adapt our product to make it more [attribute 1] and [attribute 2]? What is the impact of these attributes on product design? Packaging? Branding? How can technology enhance the perception of the positioning attributes of the product?

– **Place**: Which channels are the most adapted to reach the target? Which are compatible with the attributes of the positioning? Can we use an omnichannel strategy (reaching the target through multiple simultaneous channels)? What is the role of digital channels in our distribution strategy?

– **Price**: How does my pricing strategy affect the chosen positioning in terms of [attribute 1] and/or [attribute 2]? What is the target's price sensibility to price increase/decrease (price elasticity)? How does my pricing strategy compare to that of the nearest competitors in the positioning map? How will my pricing strategy evolve as the product matures along its life cycle curve?

– **Promotion**: Based on what we know about the target's media habits, which communication channels are the most cost-effective? What is the optimal combination of online/offline promotion? Is our sales team aware of how we are positioned and whose needs we are targeting? What is the best combination of earned versus paid digital media? Have we a search engine optimization plan? What keywords to use in our paid search engine advertising campaigns? What is our online community management plan? How can we emphasize our positioning attributes via experiential marketing initiatives involving as many of the five senses (smelling, touching, tasting, hearing, seeing) as possible?.

If the business plan concerns a service, three additional Ps must be added to the business plan:

– **People**: Are the employees who will be in contact with the target segments perfectly aware of the positioning strategy and its attributes? How can training programs enhance their role in reinforcing the positioning attributes by their gestures, speech, posture with customers? How are employees kept happy and in line with the company's vision/culture so that it translates in great customer service?

– **Process**: How can we improve the user experience and the logistics of service delivery? Have you discussed a visual representation of the customer journey with your teams? How can you improve the process to further reinforce the attributes in the positioning map? What are the implications of these attributes in managing the resources involved? Can we use Internet of Things solutions to automate interactions and increase productivity? Can we reduce your environmental impact by streamlining our process?

– **Physical environment**: Can you reinforce your positioning attributes as you design the physical spaces where the service is going to take place? How can the choice of colors, furniture and overall layout address the target's expectations concerning the positioning attributes? Can we improve customer flow to improve their user experience?

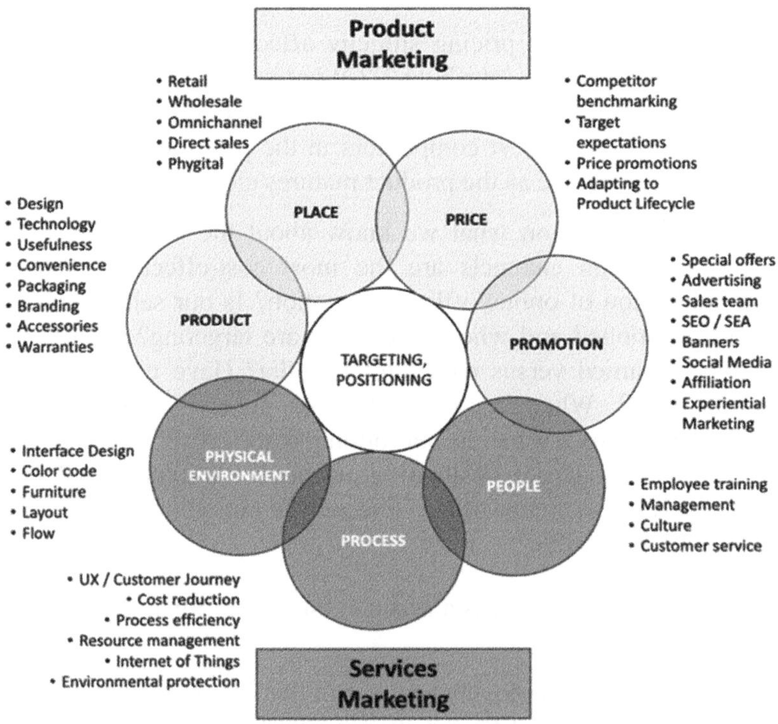

Figure 3.7. *The 4Ps of product marketing and the 3Ps of service marketing. For a color version of the figure, see http://www.iste.co.uk/lima/entrepreneurship.zip*

3.6. Organizational strengths and weaknesses

So far, students have explored opportunities and threats in the external environment, chosen a segment to target, established a competitive positioning and adjusted their marketing mix accordingly. This was an exercise of adapting variables they control (the marketing strategy and the operational marketing decisions) to those they do not control (PESTEL and competitive environments). In this section, we will further explore variables students do control in a new venture creation process: the setting up of their startup organizations.

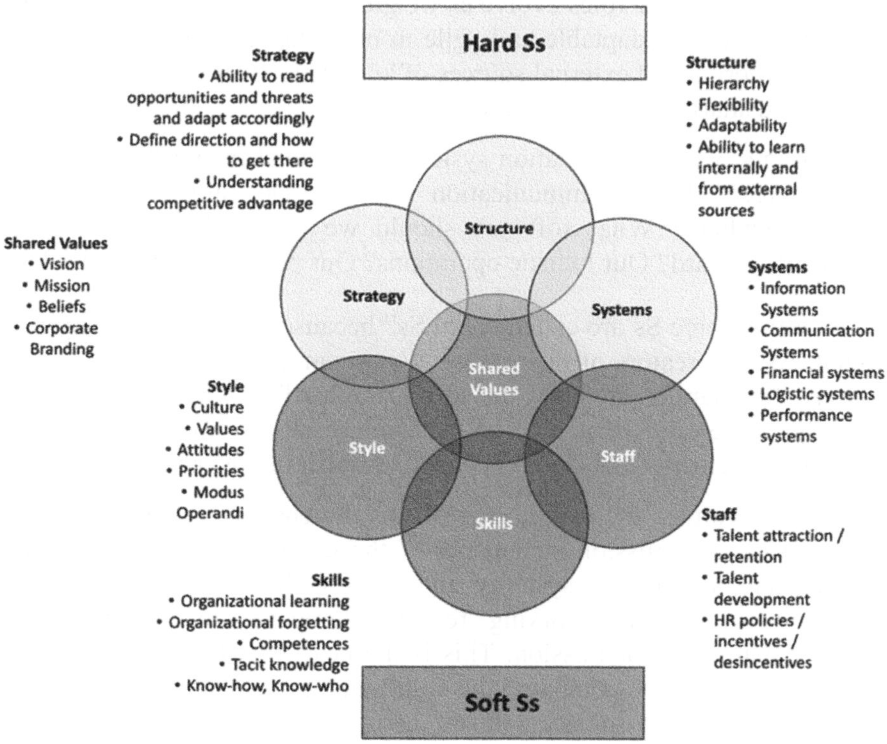

Figure 3.8. *McKinsey's 7S framework. For a color version of the figure, see http://www.iste.co.uk/lima/entrepreneurship.zip*

Most business plan templates include a section about describing the initial organizational setup. The leading consulting company McKinsey created a framework to help companies think about the multiple dimensions involved in this task: the 7S model. Such framework is presented in Figure 3.8. The following are a few questions that founders of startups could ask from the very beginning of their project in order to determine the ideal organizational setup:

– **Strategy**: who are our targets and what is our positioning? Can we address the unmet needs of a segment better than the existing competitors? What are our competitive advantages? How can we differentiate ourselves? How can we deliver a more adapted value proposition?

– **Structure**: what are the roles that each partner will play (organizational chart)? How will these roles evolve as we grow? How can we make sure that we remain flexible, adaptable and agile in order to be able to learn quickly from both internal and external sources of knowledge? How can we facilitate learning and sharing among ourselves?

– **Systems**: which information systems are crucial to run the business at startup stage? What communication systems can allow us to work anytime/anywhere? What software should we use to keep track of our financial dashboard? Our logistic operations? Our performance metrics?

These first three Ss are called "hard Ss" because they can be easily made explicit. As the creators of this model, Waterman and Peters (1980) argued, however, "the hard Ss are easy, the soft Ss are hard". By that they meant the other four dimensions that involve the unpredictability of human behavior and the tacit elements that are embedded in human minds, namely:

– **Shared values**: the visible part of this dimension is often synthesized by the vision and mission statements of the company. At a deeper level, however, are the belief systems and values that give employees the motivation to continue working for the company, by believing in a "superordinate goal" or mission. This is the heart of what will become the "brand identity" of the company, the values and promises that future clients and employees will associate with the company logo. It should be closely associated with the original vision (see Chapter 2).

– **Style**: this is organizational culture, or "the way we do things around here". It is the invisible "software" that determines the attitudes or the people in the organization environment and how they solve problems.

– **Skills**: this is what the organization knows, their core competences and the know how embedded in its employees. Understanding that core competency is essential to determine which parts of the value creation process we can delegate to third parties (partners).

– **Staff**: these are the people we hire and how we develop their talent. As one of the key components of innovative companies, this dimension involves HR practices that will keep employees happy, motivated and creative.

The original proponents of this model held that all dimensions are equally important, but the theory of disruption by Clayton Christensen, as we will see later, suggests otherwise. Indeed, companies like Nokia and Blackberry had great staff, a flexible structure, state-of-the-art systems, skills and management styles, yet failed because their strategy (sticking to keyboard based phones several years after Apple introduced the iPhone in 2007) was flawed. We will discuss this model in more detail in Chapter 6, when we present it as a knowledge management framework for scaling up startups while remaining innovative. Business model strategy will be the main topic of the next chapter.

3.7. Other sources of competitive strengths and weaknesses

Porter's Value Chain model (1980) is very complementary to McKinsey's 7S in helping students think about variables they control in the internal organizational environment. It divides typical organizational functions in two domains: the primary activities that directly create value and the secondary activities that do so indirectly (see Figure 3.9). Primary activities involve everything that is directly related to product or service delivery, from the supply chain (inbound logistics) to the transformation operations, through distribution (outbound logistics), marketing and after-sales services. The secondary activities have to do with resource management that contribute indirectly to the core business: legal, financial and material resources (infrastructure), human resources, knowledge/learning/innovation resources and external resources (procurement).

In their business plan, students should look at each one of these dimensions as a source of strengths or weaknesses. This is going to prove very useful in the next stage.

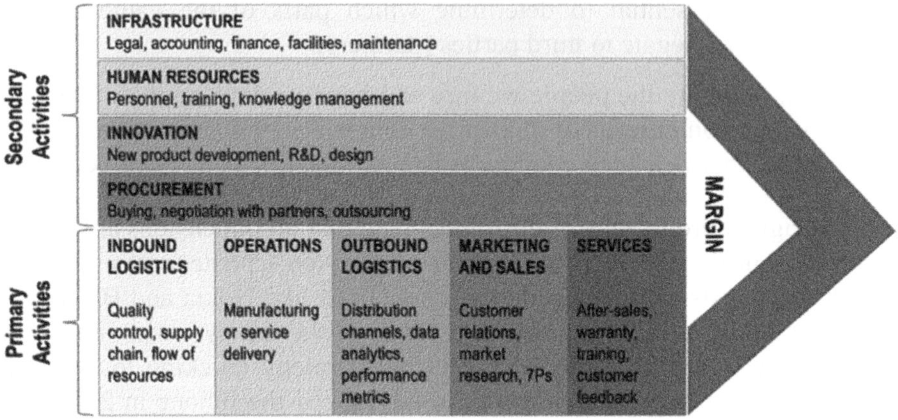

Figure 3.9. *Value Chain model (adapted from Porter 1980). For a color version of the figure, see http://www.iste.co.uk/lima/entrepreneurship.zip*

3.8. Strategy and development plan: the TOWS matrix

By now, students have systematically worked on all aspects of the external and internal environments of their new venture, thanks to the extensive checklists provided above. It is now time to extract meaningful plans of action based on those insights. One of the most common mistakes business school students make is to describe strengths and weaknesses, opportunities and threats in an inert SWOT list that does not deal with the fundamental question at stake here: the "*So what?*" question. How should they use their strengths to take advantage of the opportunities? How should they minimize their weaknesses in order to avoid major threats?

The TOWS matrix analysis (Figure 3.10) should help them do just that. One of its merits is its synthetic power: only the most important external and internal forces should be listed here. So, their first task is to re-read all the work done in the above sections of the business plan and to isolate, from their PESTEL-C analysis, three to five opportunities (duly labeled O1, O2, etc.) and a similar number of threats (T1, T2, …, Tn). Then, they must go over the marketing strategy (STP framework), operational marketing plan (7P), organizational setup (7S) and activities of the firm (value chain) in search of the most relevant strengths (S1, S2, …, Sn) and weaknesses (W1, W2, …, Wn). This nomenclature will make it easier to trace back the decisions in the TOWS matrix later.

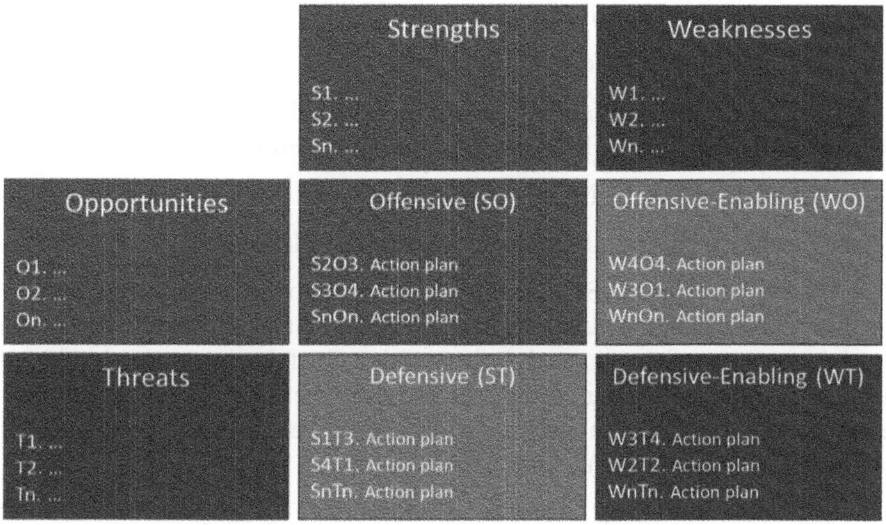

Figure 3.10. *TOWS matrix with offensive and defensive strategies. For a color version of the figure, see http://www.iste.co.uk/lima/entrepreneurship.zip*

It is very important that each action plan starts with a verb. Below is an example of a short TOWS analysis based on the following SWOT[1] about a Lebanese craft beer company:

– Strengths (S), Weaknesses (W):

- S1. Entrepreneurial spirit of the founder, passion for his or her profession;

- S2. Knowledge of the local market;

- S3. Handcrafted quality with an industrial scale;

- S4. Strong organizational culture and capacity for innovation;

- W1. Regional brand, little international visibility;

- W2. Difficulty accessing distribution networks;

- W3. Limited resources;

1 Adapted from a case study in my book about case analysis using frameworks (Lima and Fabiani 2014).

– Opportunities (O), Threats (T):

- O1. Starting craft beer in Lebanon;

- O2. Wave of ecological awareness adapted to the development of a craft beer T1. Competitor beer market monopoly (international group);

- T2. Political instability;

- T3. Weak culture of alcoholic beverages in Lebanon.

– **Offensive actions (SO)**. Building on its innovative spirit (S1 and S4), the entrepreneur should reinforce the image of "first craft beer" by creating special aromas and a "limited series editions" of its beers. It should also strengthen its positioning as an "ecological beer" by communicating its artisanal quality (S3) in order to attract more consumers sensitive to environmental issues (O2).

– **Offensive-enabling actions (WO)**. The entrepreneur's limited resources (W3) do not allow the creation of massive communication campaigns to strengthen the positioning of the brand as "Lebanon's first craft beer"; he or she must therefore use social networks to strengthen the sense of community of "statutory, connoisseurs" of beer, offering exclusive content on the craft process and tips for tasting his or her exceptional beer.

– **Defensive actions (ST)**. In order to minimize the power of the competitor (subsidiary of a multinational) Almaza (T1) and the risk of lower internal sales due to political instability (T2), Hajjar must use its unique positioning the first Lebanese craft beer to export its product to the most demanding beer markets in the world, notably Europe, the United States and Latin America. It could target several communities of the "Lebanese diaspora" in these regions to offer them a "taste of the fatherland" at a premium price, appealing to their deep sense of national identity.

– **Defensive-enabling actions (WT)**. In order to circumvent the weak culture of alcoholic beverages in Lebanon (T3) and its modest international reputation (W1), the entrepreneur could strengthen its line of non-alcoholic beers for export to the Arab world. As they have limited resources (W3), they should create strategic partnerships for the international distribution of this product line, thus minimizing its difficulty of access to channels (W2).

If done well, a TOWS matrix allows entrepreneurs not only to prioritize the most important forces affecting their business but also to make strategic decisions which can be easily traceable back to their external and internal sources.

3.9. Financial objectives

The best way to deal with the several financial objectives in a business plan is to make use of online spreadsheet templates, which are readily available through a Google search. One good example of a website dedicated to sharing free templates to develop financial reports for startups is Score.org[2]. The following is a list of the templates presented there:

– startup expenses;

– payroll costs;

– sales forecast;

– operating expenses for the first three years in business;

– cash flow statements for the first three years in business;

– income statements for the first three years in business;

– balance sheet;

– break-even analysis;

– financial ratios;

– cost of goods sold (COGS);

– amortization and depreciation for your business.

They also have marketing and sales templates that could be equally useful. Score.org is a non-profit association whose objective it is to facilitate the creation of startups around the world.

3.10. Conclusions and perspectives

This final part is optional. It consists of reiterating what the opportunity is and why the entrepreneur is well positioned to seize it. The authors can highlight here how they are aware of the main threats in their way and how they intend to minimize them. Above all, they could use this section to create a Gantt chart with the main stages of their business development plan, mentioning milestones in their project management strategy and clear metrics of success along their path. A quick online search for "Gantt chart templates" will give you an idea of the various readily available resources

2 https://www.score.org/resource/business-planning-financial-statements-template-gallery.

for creating your own chart. The website https://clickup.com/blog/free-gantt-chart-software/ lists 12 such free (or freemium) online solutions. They also have a detailed explanation of typical chart components, such as milestones, breakdown structure and critical path.

3.11. Appendices and References

The final part of a business plan includes appendices and references. In the appendices, students can place all kinds of diagrams, pictures and exhibits that would be too voluminous and distracting to be included in the main text. They can also use any primary data collection tools used (questionnaires with potential targets, interview guides with partners and stakeholders, etc.). In the references, they should list all the secondary data sources consulted: websites, databases, academic articles, press stories, market analysis sources, etc. We suggest the use of the APA (American Psychological Association) standard, which is the most widely used for in-text citations and full bibliographic references.

3.12. Teaching business planning

If you know the enemy and know yourself, you need not fear the result of a hundred battles. If you know yourself but not the enemy, for every victory gained you will also suffer a defeat. If you know neither the enemy nor yourself, you will succumb in every battle.

Sun Tzu,
The Art of War

The most important role teachers can have while teaching business plan tools is to make sure that students are clear about both the view of the "forest" and the "trees". Students tend to get lost in the different analytical steps and often fail to establish a clear connection between them. Helping them understand the underlying thread is paramount.

One way of doing this is by clearly establishing the difference between the elements the entrepreneur does not control (opportunities and threats in the environment) and the ones they do control (strengths and weaknesses in their marketing strategy, organization design and financial planning). It is not enough to simply enumerate these external and internal variables, however. It is important to understand how they are interrelated.

3.12.1. *Reflecting about the frameworks in a business plan*

The TOWS matrix is an excellent exercise in articulating controllable and uncontrollable factors in a business plan. A whole 18-hour discipline can be created around a project to develop a very elaborate matrix. The class would start by explaining the difference between TOWS and SWOT. To illustrate the difference between controllable and uncontrollable elements of the TOWS, the market analysis scheme presented in Figure 3.10 could be a good starting point, with the first layer presenting sources of opportunities and threats (PESTEL checklist, the competitive environment, main market trends arising from market research). The second and third layers present sources of strengths and weaknesses in the marketing strategy (segmentation, targeting and positioning) and in the marketing plan (4Ps or 7Ps of the marketing mix). The 7S model and the Value Chain model should be also discussed as other sources of strengths and weaknesses. Finally, the financial plan itself can have positive elements (quick return over investment, low funding requirements, initial investor) as well as potential weaknesses (unpredictable sales growth, extended negative cash flow for several months, etc.).

3.12.2. *Creating and authentic business plan environment*

The discussion of the above frameworks should not be done academically but pragmatically applying them to each student's own business ideas. In short, they should develop the business plan *during* the semester. Each new class could start with a few volunteer students presenting how they are applying the tools discussed in the previous class, followed by feedback, questions and comments both from the teacher and from the fellow students. In order to contextualize each project, a short presentation of the executive summary would be required. The teacher may also ask volunteers about their strategies to develop a literature review and stimulate them to use databases to find key trends, competitive information and market data.

3.12.3. *Using technology to make it more interactive and collaborative*

In order to keep track of student business plans as they are being developed, it is a good idea to have an online spreadsheet presenting the links to individual reports. This shared document could make it easier for students to get peer reviews of each step of their progress. Figure 3.11 presents an example of how such a sheet could be structured.

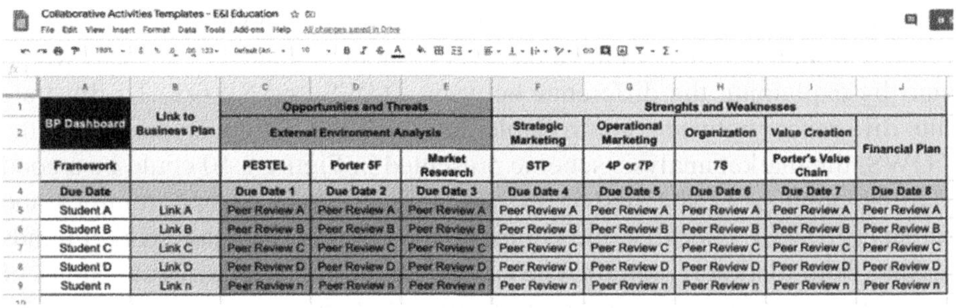

BP Dashboard	Link to Business Plan	Opportunities and Threats			Strenghts and Weaknesses				
		External Environment Analysis			Strategic Marketing	Operational Marketing	Organization	Value Creation	Financial Plan
Framework		PESTEL	Porter 5F	Market Research	STP	4P or 7P	7S	Porter's Value Chain	
Due Date		Due Date 1	Due Date 2	Due Date 3	Due Date 4	Due Date 5	Due Date 6	Due Date 7	Due Date 8
Student A	Link A	Peer Review A	Peer Review A	Peer Review A	Peer Review A	Peer Review A	Peer Review A	Peer Review A	Peer Review A
Student B	Link B	Peer Review B	Peer Review B	Peer Review B	Peer Review B	Peer Review B	Peer Review B	Peer Review B	Peer Review B
Student C	Link C	Peer Review C	Peer Review C	Peer Review C	Peer Review C	Peer Review C	Peer Review C	Peer Review C	Peer Review C
Student D	Link D	Peer Review D	Peer Review D	Peer Review D	Peer Review D	Peer Review D	Peer Review D	Peer Review D	Peer Review D
Student n	Link n	Peer Review n	Peer Review n	Peer Review n	Peer Review n	Peer Review n	Peer Review n	Peer Review n	Peer Review n

Figure 3.11. *Example of a Google Docs shared sheet as a peer-review dashboard. For a color version of the figure, see http://www.iste.co.uk/lima/entrepreneurship.zip*

Teachers should first create the template using an online platform such as Google Docs or Microsoft 365. Then, they must change the sharing settings in this document in such a way that "anybody with the link may edit it". This step is a bit tricky. Students can easily misuse the power to edit a collaborative sheet to vandalize the collective work or to post pranks anonymously. There are two ways of dealing with this scenario: the easiest one is to trust the maturity of students to respect each other's work. I have used this approach for the past seven years without any problems. I often remind students of Spider Man's philosophy: "with great power comes great responsibility".

The second approach involves breaking anonymity. Instead of using the setting "anybody with the link may edit" the sheet, teachers could use the option "invite nominal users" and send them a personal invitation requiring them to log in and identify themselves. If the school uses a corporate solution such as Google's G-suit or Microsoft's Office 365 platform, all students will have school credentials in the platform and teachers can use the option "only people in my organization may edit this".

The easiest way to share the link to the collaborative sheet is to use a URL shortening service such as bit.ly or ow.ly. These free services convert a long, unruly web address into a more blackboard-friendly version that looks like, for example, bit.ly/FyUi2A or ow.ly/GhYT3b.

In the example depicted in Figure 3.11, students can list their own names in column A (the teacher can later sort them alphabetically). A simple peer-review rule can be established, such as Student B will peer-review Student A's work, Student C will review Student B's work and so on, with Student n reviewing Student A's work. Peer reviews should be kept short (one paragraph at the most), with questions and comments that can help each colleague go further in his or her reflection.

Students can be taught how to use a URL shortener and how to configure sharing settings to their own online documents, which they can paste in column B. At the very least, each online document should contain a draft of the executive summary in order to contextualize the business plan idea from day one.

Columns C and D have each a specific due date for the opportunities and threats deliverables (PESTEL, competitive forces and market research). Columns F–I contain the deadlines for the strengths and weaknesses deliverables and the peer reviews that go with them. The final due date concerns the financial plan (column J).

4

From Business Plan to Business Model

No plan ever survives its first encounter with the enemy.

Douglas MacArthur,
American general in World War II

Twenty years ago, when students came to an entrepreneurship teacher with a new venture idea, the first thing they would be told was "develop your business plan". Such a plan would often consist, among other things, of a marketing strategy, an organizational structure, cash flow requirements and (often overestimated) return over investment and break-even point spreadsheets, as seen above.

In the early 2000s, the advent of the World Wide Web, data-driven processes and wider ecosystem interdependence all contributed to increasing the complexity of entrepreneurial decisions. If business plans were hardly adapted as a strategic tool for decision-making before this digital transformation, criticism against static plans only grew with the speed and complexity of the information age. According to Mullins and Komisar (2010, p. 1),

> [t]he typical startup process, whether in nascent entrepreneurial ventures or in the innovation units of established businesses, is largely driven by poorly conceived business plans based on

> untested assumptions. This process is seriously flawed. Most new ventures, even those with venture capital or corporate backing, share one common characteristic: They fail. There is a better way to launch new ideas – without wasting years of time and loads of investors' money. This better way is about discovering a business model that really works.

This criticism highlights the main limitations of traditional business plans: they often rely on "untested assumptions" about product desirability and feasibility and fail because they lack the built-in mechanisms for dynamic evolution. The business model approach, described in this chapter, is based on the premise that every assumption must be tested in an iterative process of "learning-by-trying". Business model designers understand that their ability to create value does not derive necessarily from the technology they use. As Chesbrough (2010) argues, it is better to have a mediocre technology with a great business model than the opposite.

All these cautionary arguments do not mean that business plans have become completely obsolete, only that the expectations have changed. Instead of trusting a business plan to accurately reflect the medium- and long-term scenarios for a new venture, most investors and educators tend to look at it as an exercise in knowledge building about the market, the competitors and the initial strategic choices. Both investors and entrepreneurship educators expect students to go beyond a descriptive business plan: they must iteratively develop a business *model*. In this sense, business plans and business models can be complementary in entrepreneurship education.

The following sections describe a business model artifact that help entrepreneurs think about the dynamic elements of their value creation process. The first two parts of this section are rather theoretical and are aimed at teachers wishing to better understand the origins and the cognitive benefits of the Business Model Canvas. Students may wish to skip these topics and go straight to section 4.3.

4.1. Business models and business model artifacts[1]

Even though the origins of the term "business model" (BM) can be traced back to the 1950s and 1960s, it rose to prominence towards the end of the 20th Century with the advent of the Internet as a new means to create, distribute and capture value (Teece 2010; Zott *et al.* 2011; Günzel and Holm 2013; Rodet-Kroichvili *et al.* 2014). In spite of lacking a common definition (Verstraete *et al.* 2012), there is a growing consensus around the notion that business models as "the rationale of how an organization creates, delivers and captures value" (Osterwalder and Pigneur 2010, p. 14). Value is created by the management of resources (human, informational, financial and material) around key activities that allow organizations to provide a value proposition. This value proposition is delivered through digital and physical channels that reach the unmet needs of customers, who are prepared to pay for such value with their loyalty, influence and cash. Such is synthetically the flow of value creation, delivery and capture in a typical business model.

Thus, a BM represents the conceptual link between strategy, business organization and systems to create, deliver and capture value (Johnson *et al.* 2008). It can also be abstractly defined as "the means by which a firm creates and sustains margins of growth" (Euchner and Ganguly 2014, p. 33) or "the heuristic logic that connects technical potential with the realization of economic value" (Chesbrough and Rosenbloom 2002, p. 529). Or, more concretely, as a framework that "articulates the logic, the data and other evidence that support a value proposition for the customer, and a viable structure of revenues and costs for the enterprise delivering that value" (Teece 2010, p. 179). Eppler *et al.* (2011) describe the role of BM frameworks as artifacts that facilitate group ideation and innovation processes. In this sense, BM artifacts can be templates, sketches and other materials that are used to test ideas and foster collaboration (Verstraete *et al.* 2012).

Templates and frameworks for analyzing business ideas and visualizing concepts have long been part of managerial practice. As we have previously seen, Michael Porter (1980, 1985, 1990) contributed with several such visual tools for strategic analysis as his ubiquitous Five Forces and Value Chain

1 Certain excerpts of this chapter have been adapted from published articles by the author (see Lima and Baudier 2017 and Lima *et al.* 2018).

models. In another example, Kaplan and Norton (1992) define their Balanced Scorecard as a control panel representing a visually intuitive strategic planning and management system (see Chapter 6). Those artifacts are supposed to facilitate collaboration and visual communication of structured ideas, thus creating "checklists for thinking" about the multiple dimensions involved in business problem solving and how these dimensions are conceptually linked (Ten Have *et al.* 2003; Lima and Fabiani 2014). Verstraete *et al.* (2012) emphasize the systemic nature of these artifacts, pointing out that each component or sub-system of a visual artifact is heuristically linked to the others.

Several attempts have been made to create visual descriptions of BM components. Bouwman *et al.* (2008) propose a service-based model with a focus on technology design and innovation. Johnson *et al.* (2008) created a simplified four-dimension sketch involving customer value proposition, profit formula, key processes and key resources. Pynnonen *et al.* (2012) designed a "Business Mapping Framework" to trace the value-stream structure of value networks. Abdelkafi *et al.* (2013) conceived a six-dimensional template consisting of value proposition, creation, communication, capture, dissemination and development. Cavalcante (2014) suggests three central components in a framework: value creation, *modus operandi* and value capture mechanisms. According to that author, these components should be developed in three phases: defining the core processes, identifying change requirements and addressing the challenges created by those changes. Jouison and Verstraete (2008) propose a three-stage visual artifact that describes the generation, remuneration and sharing of value creation processes. It is interesting to note the apparent influence of the Business Model Canvas (Osterwalder and Pigneur, 2010) on the work of Verstraete. In their earlier work, Jouison and Verstraete (2008) described a complex framework to explain the impact of business models on strategic thinking; more recently, their nine-block matrix is followed by a more icon-based artifact that makes it easier to visualize and manipulate the elements of a business model (Verstraete *et al.* 2011, 2012).

Our decision to focus our study on Osterwalder's Business Model artifact in this book rather than any of the above alternatives has to do with the fact that the BMC is the most widely adopted academic framework for BM innovation both among students and practitioners (Blank 2013). Therefore, if we can understand which factors lead students in a nation-wide entrepreneurship program to adopt this tool, this study could become a steppingstone to understanding the use of this artifact in a larger community of startups and innovative companies in future studies.

4.2. Claimed benefits and criticism of the BMC

Despite the emergence of several alternatives to their initial insight over the past few years, the original Business Model Canvas by Osterwalder and Pigneur (2010) remains arguably the most widely used artifact for business modeling (Müller and Thoring 2012; Blank 2013). The BMC is constituted by nine building blocks derived from an in-depth literature review conducted by Alexander Osterwalder (2004) during his doctorate at Lausanne University under the supervision of Yves Pigneur. Influenced by their Information Systems backgrounds, the proponents intended it to be perceived as an ontological framework for clearly defined relationships between the components (Figure 4.1).

The right side of the canvas emphasizes choosing, delivering and capturing value using five building blocks: customer segments, value proposition, channels, customer relations, revenue streams. The left side is focused on value creation through internal and external processes and logistics using four blocks: key activities, key resources, key partnerships and costs. The value proposition building block is the centerpiece of the canvas. Business model innovation ideas are obtained by brainstorming the contents of each building block, using highly visual tools such as sticky notes, doodles and diagrams (Fritscher and Pigneur 2010; Eppler *et al.* 2011).

Business model literature is pervaded by implicit or explicit claims about the potential benefits associated with using artifacts or templates for business model innovation. Table 4.1 summarizes the main claimed advantages of defining a clear business model (BM). One may think of claimed benefits 1 through 3 (performance, communication, innovation) primarily as "functional" or "organizational" benefits, as they affect a firm's overall ability to function in a competitive environment. These are more closely associated with the organizational environment rather than the cognitive process of business modeling. Conversely, one may refer to the other five claims (visualization, decision-making, creative thinking, collaboration and reflection) primarily as "cognitive" benefits or tasks. These are related to the way BM artifacts are expected to facilitate the process of reasoning rather than the organizational output.

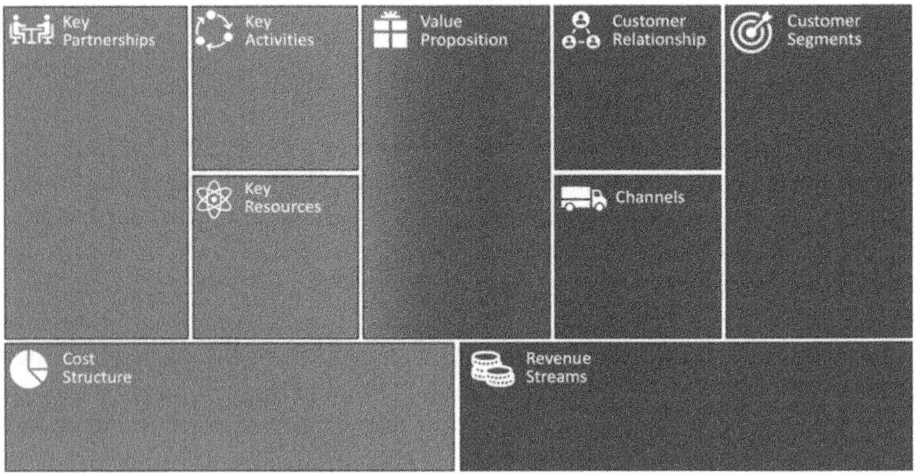

Figure 4.1. *The Business Model Canvas (adapted from Osterwalder and Pigneur, 2010). For a color version of the figure, see http://www.iste.co.uk/lima/entrepreneurship.zip*

This division of expected results in terms of cognitive and functional benefits is consistent with the premise that the BMC is essentially an instrument for making individual and collaborative decisions about organizational effectiveness (Mintzberg 1989). The perceived benefits on both the cognitive and organizational domains address the question of why users ultimately adopt this tool: because they expect it to contribute in terms of *efficacy* (a better performing organization which can improve its innovation strategy and effectively communicate it to stakeholders) and *efficiency* (better processes for visually manipulating the variables involved in individual and collaborative decision-making).

The hegemony of the BMC is not without criticism, however. As Euchner and Ganguly (2014, p. 35) stated, "Strong business models cannot be generated by brainstorming the elements of a business model using a tool like the Business Model Canvas." According to them, the BMC does not represent well the coherence or relationships among the elements. It also fails to represent strategic items such as the competitive position of the firm and the economic and the economic leverage points. De Reuver *et al.* (2013) also note that the BMC simplicity is both a strength, because it is readily applicable, and weakness because it provides little detail about each variable. Conversely, Günzel and Holm (2013) mention that the multifaceted structure of the BMC may create "perplexities and complexities" in the business model innovation process. Eppler *et al.* (2011) found that while the BMC could enhance collaboration, it could also have a negative impact on perceived creativity during the ideation process due to the fixed structure of the template. Fritscher and Pigneur (2010) recognize that highly structured templates such as the BMC must be carefully designed to offer enough specialized functionality to emphasize general thinking guidelines without compromising free thought and creativity.

Claimed benefits		**Sources**
Functional benefits (related to the expected *organizational outputs* of BM innovation activities)	1. Performance	Zott and Amit 2007, 2008; Trimi and Berbegal-Mirabent 2012; Verstraete *et al.* 2012; Gunzel and Holm 2013
	2. Communication	Osterwalder *et al.* 2005; Jouison and Verstraete 2008; Fritscher and Pigneur 2010; Trimi and Berbegal-Mirabent 2012
	3. Innovation	Johnson *et al.* 2008; Chesborough 2010; Teece 2010; Zott *et al.* 2011
Cognitive benefits (related to the *thinking process* of individuals and groups using the BM as an innovation tool)	4. Visualization	Osterwalder *et al.* 2005; Fritscher and Pigneur 2010; Osterwalder and Pigneur 2010; Verstraete *et al.* 2012
	5. Decision-making	Osterwalder and Pigneur 2010; Trimi and Berbegal-Mirabent 2012; Schneider and Spieth 2014
	6. Creative thinking	Fritscher and Pigneur 2010; Eppler *et al.* 2011; Schneider and Spieth 2014
	7. Collaboration	Fritcher and Pigneur 2010; Osterwalder and Pigneur 2010; Eppler *et al.* 2011; Verstraete *et al.* 2012
	8. Reflection	Teece 2010; Trimi and Berbegal-Mirabent 2012; Schneider and Spieth 2013

Table 4.1. *Claimed benefits of business model artifacts*

These objections and limitations do not seem to affect the growing popularity of the BMC. In the following sections, we will describe each one of the components of Osterwalder's framework and how they combine to establish a "rationale of value creation, delivery and capture".

4.3. Value flow in the Business Model Canvas

The BMC can be very misleading in the way it represents value flows. Indeed, the left-to-right disposition of the value-creation > value delivery > value capture approach may lead students to start their business modeling on the left side of the canvas. Starting from the left would not be a consistent way of presenting their value chain, as it does not make sense to talk about partners, activities and resources (i.e. how we create value) *before* we talk about segments and value proposition (i.e. what value we are creating and for whom). Figure 4.2 suggests a sequence of logical flow for presenting the process of value delivery. It is based on an earlier work of the designers of the Business Model Canvas (before the publication of Osterwalder's book in 2010). It draws on Osterwalder's doctorate thesis (defended in 2004), which emphasizes the notion of "ontology". In Information Science, an ontology is the visual representation of categories, properties and relations between concepts.

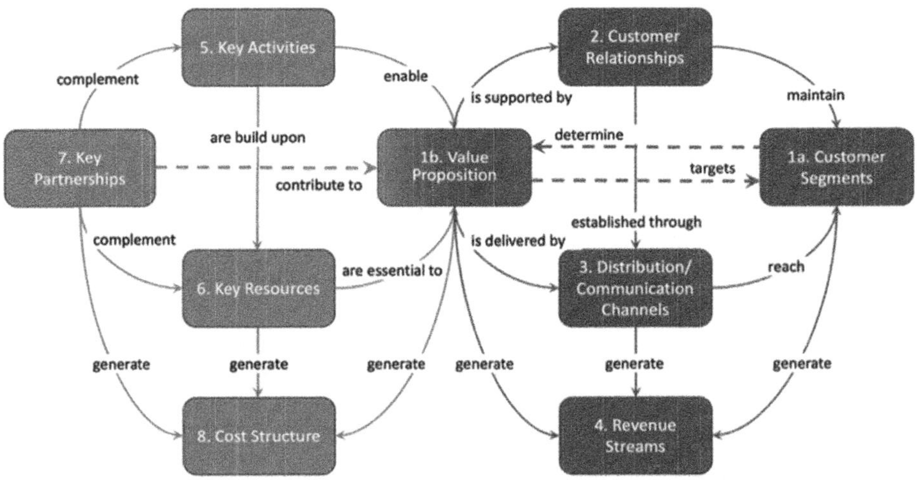

Figure 4.2. *Value flow in the ontology diagram of the Business Model Canvas (adapted from Fritscher and Pigneur 2010). For a color version of the figure, see http://www.iste.co.uk/lima/entrepreneurship.zip*

We adapted their diagram to illustrate the natural sequence of value creation: first, one must address the questions of "whose unmet needs do we wish to address?" (1a. customer segments) and "what are the main differentiating attributes of our product/service?" (1b. value proposition). It makes more sense to identify a need and to fulfill it with a product than to develop a product and then search for a need (the proverbial solution in search of a problem).

Yet, several entrepreneurs make the basic mistake of falling into Ralph Waldo Emerson's so-called "mousetrap fallacy". The 19th Century American philosopher is credited with having stated that "if you build a better mousetrap, the world will beat a path to your door". This dangerous belief is based on the premise that a very good product or service will market itself. Common among engineers, this assumption leads to "technology-push" innovations, that is, products designed according to what the designers believe to be the problem and the ideal solution. Sometimes, technology-push solutions do work. Steve Jobs famously launched the iPhone with no market research data to confirm that touch screens would be a superior solution than keyboards on a smartphone. However, for every iPhone, there are thousands of failed products which were designed with very little regard towards real-world needs and expectations.

The opposite approach, illustrated in Figure 4.3, is known as "market pull". It assumes that one must understand the unmet need and the target before you can position your product. Only after the targeting and positioning is clear can you develop the product/service and then source/manufacture it and then market it. We have discussed this approach in the previous chapter. McKinsey consultants Lanning and Michaels (1988) call this market-pull approach a "Value Delivery System". Choosing the value (the process of determining whose unmet needs they are going to address) is arguably the most important decision an entrepreneur will make. Their choice of target and positioning will affect what they make, how they make it and how they deliver and communicate it.

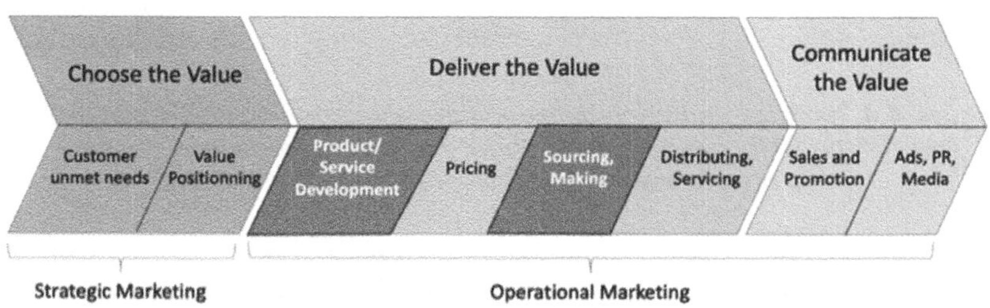

Figure 4.3. *Value delivery system (adapted from Lanning and Michaels 1988). For a color version of the figure, see http://www.iste.co.uk/lima/entrepreneurship.zip*

As Fristscher and Pigneur's ontology above demonstrates, however, most modern innovation processes are a constant iteration of technology push and market pull. It is indeed important for an entrepreneur to understand what they do well (their "core competence") and what they are passionate about (see Filion's Visionary Model in Chapter 2). They need to understand the ecosystem, the resources and technology intensive activities necessary for value creation. But if they ignore who can be best served by that competence and what attributes are the most valued by that target (positioning), they may end up developing a product or service that no one cares about. Studies indicate that between 40% and 90% of new products fail (depending on the category). According to Gourville (2006), out of 30,000 new packaged goods introduced in the USA every year, more than 70% are aborted less than 12 months after their launch. The iterative spiral approach for value creation and delivery illustrated in Figure 4.4 should drastically improve the probability of designing a solution that customers actually need based on the competences/resources we excel in.

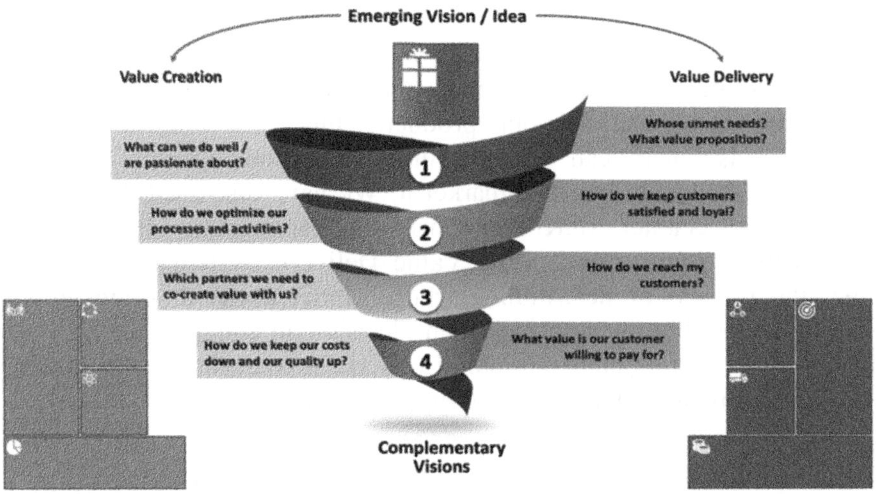

Figure 4.4. *Iterative approach between the value creation and value delivery sides of the BMC (source: the author). For a color version of the figure, see http://www.iste.co.uk/lima/entrepreneurship.zip*

While developing the business model, the entrepreneur will have to oscillate between the value creation and value delivery sides as they mature their initial idea.

4.3.1. *Delivering and capturing value: the right side of the canvas*

The right side of the canvas is about delivering the expected value to selected targets, allowing organizations to generate revenue (value capture). It is also about making sure that these transactions are perpetuated in time, by creating loyalty and recursive purchases. As illustrated in Figure 4.4, the right side of the canvas deals with the following questions:

1) **Customer segments and value proposition**. For whom are we creating value? Which segments should we target? What do I need to know about these segments to better understand their needs? What are the unmet needs of this segment concerning my product/service? What attributes (functional, social, emotional) does this segment expect me to emphasize in my product/service development? These two categories are inseparable and should be considered iteratively. Any idea for a value proposition development should be tested with the targeted segments and validated according to their needs/expectations.

2) **Customer relationship**. How do I keep my customer satisfied and loyal to my brand? How do I use data and digital technologies to learn more about their needs? How can we listen to their feedback?

3) **Channels**. How do I reach my target audience (both in terms of logistics/distribution) as in terms of communication (promotion)? What is the role of digital technology in both logistics (omnichannel solutions) and communication (digital marketing tools)?

4) **Revenue streams**. How do we capture the value we have created? How much are customers willing to pay for that value? What other benefits can I get from offering my value proposition (data, brand loyalty)?

Another way to read the ontological categories of the right side of the canvas could be thus: the value proposition emerges from understanding the unmet need of targeted customers and how we are uniquely positioned to address them. In order to maintain these customers' loyalty, we need to establish customer relationship mechanisms (community management, loyalty schemes, gamification, direct marketing) that will allow us to keep in touch with these customers while getting to know them better (data analysis). To reach our customers, our communication strategy requires both digital (website, social media, newsletters) and physical (stores, distribution partners, printed media) channels. These channels are used not only for communication but also for the delivery of our products and services. If we deliver value appropriately, customers will be happy to reward us with their cash and loyalty.

Figure 4.5 establishes a relationship between the 7Ps of Marketing discussed in Chapter 3 and the right side of the Business Model Canvas. As we can see, all the elements of operational marketing fit in the Canvas. The Value Proposition should encapsulate key attributes of the product or service as well as its positioning strategy. As in the 7Ps model, all marketing decisions should be based on the choice of positioning and targets (Customer segments): which communication channels to use (promotion), which distribution networks to exploit (place), how to design the shops, buildings where service delivery happens (physical environment), how to enhance the customer experience to improve brand loyalty (processes), how to train the employees who will translate the company values when in contact with customers (people) and how to adjust the expected level of revenue streams (price).

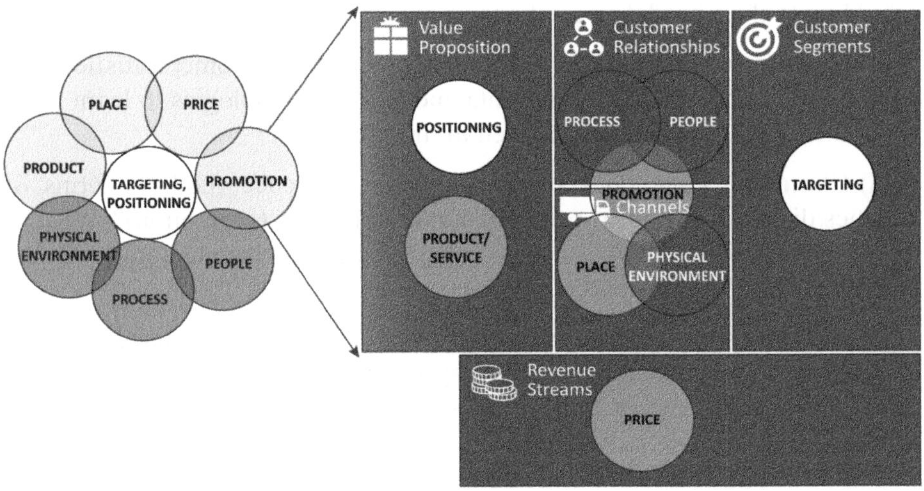

Figure 4.5. *Equivalence between 7P framework and the right side of the BMC. For a color version of the figure, see http://www.iste.co.uk/lima/entrepreneurship.zip*

4.3.2. *Creating value and controlling costs: the left side of the canvas*

The left side of the canvas is about the operational and logistic decisions that often escape marketing specialists, but which are essential to create value. They elicit questions about the following:

1) **Key activities**. What are we good at/knowledgeable/passionate about (core competences)? Which one of these activities are essential to create the value proposition? Which aspects of these processes differentiate us from the competition?

2) **Key resources**. In order to perform the essential activities that create the value proposition, which talent profiles are essential? Which technological resources are strategic? Are there any intangible resources (brand, data, information, knowledge) we need to reinforce?

3) **Key partners**. Which aspects of the value creation process should we outsource? What are the competences (manufacturing, software development, advertising) we do not have in-house which are essential for creating the value proposition?

4) **Cost structure**. Which of the elements above (activities, resources, partnerships) are going to be most cost-intensive and need to be carefully monitored/controlled? How can we reduce these costs without affecting the expected quality?

Following the ontological categories of Figure 4.2, we have the following value-creating rationale: key activities (such as research and development, platform maintenance, product design) are built upon rare and valuable resources (talented engineers, developers, designers, marketers, as well as technical know-how, brand image, etc.). No one company can possibly create value alone: they outsource part of their activities to specialists (key partners such as manufacturers, advertisers, service providers, logistical platforms, digital platforms). All three elements (activities, resources and partners) will cost money, but if well controlled, the overall cost structure will be inferior to the revenue streams, creating a sustainable business model.

4.3.3. *Color-coding multiple-sided business models*

When targeting one single customer segment with the same expectations and needs, business model designers should use same-color "sticky notes" throughout the canvas. More complex business model structures, however, may require color-coding the value delivery process to highlight different value propositions, which may be distributed through different channels, to reach different targets, creating distinct categories of revenue streams. These are called multiple-sided business models. Take the example of Google's search engine business model depicted in Figure 4.6.

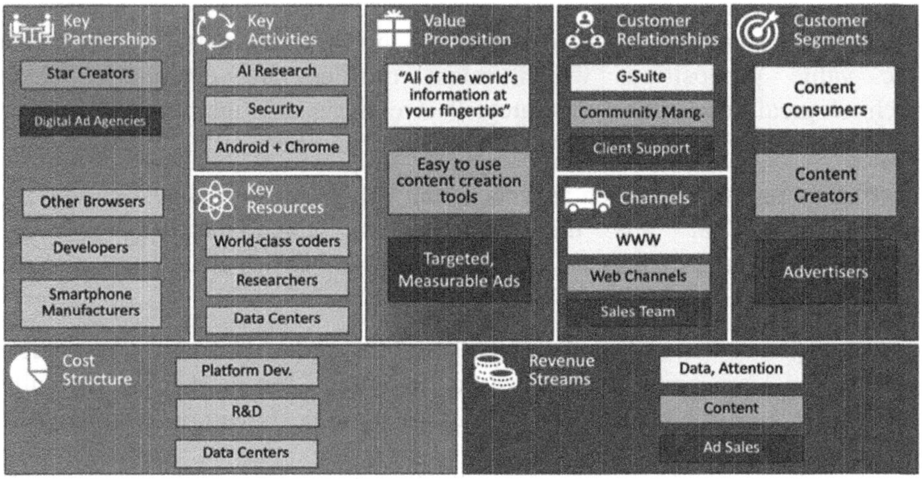

Figure 4.6. *An example of a color-coded multiple-sided business model: Google Search (created by the author). For a color version of the figure, see http://www.iste.co.uk/lima/entrepreneurship.zip*

In order to create value for advertisers, Google needs to attract a large number of web content consumers. Content consumers will not be engaged unless there is a large number of content creators posting YouTube videos, blogs, sites, news, etc. Therefore, Google needs to create three separate value propositions for each of these segments: easily accessible information for content consumers, content creation tools for creators and a targeted ad platform for advertisers. Advertisers require a specific sales channel and a specific customer support. It also requires an extensive partnership network of digital advertising solution prescribers. The only monetary revenue stream comes from advertisers who buy AdWords and AdSense products, but one may consider the data created by content consumers and the content generated by content creators as indirect assets to be monetized. Most of the other elements in the model (resources, activities, cost) are shared by the three value creation streams, and thus can be depicted in a neutral color.

4.4. Sources of business model innovation

Kline and Rosenberg (1986) differentiate between incremental (evolutionary) and radical (revolutionary) innovation. The first category comprises small, cumulative changes that may reduce costs, improve performance or better adapt a product to market expectations. The radical kind, much rarer, represents new-to-the-world, new-industry-forming innovations such as the first airplane (which created the aerospace industry), semiconductors (which gave birth to the digital revolution) and genetic engineering. Between the extremely incremental and the extremely radical types of innovation, there is a spectrum of increasingly complex technological breakthroughs.

4.4.1. *Tidd's innovation wheel*

Joe Tidd and John Bessant have synthesized the most common types of incremental and radical innovations in a 4P framework, illustrated in Figure 4.7:

– Product or service innovation is about "what we do". Typically, incremental product innovations include changing the shape or packaging of a product to make it easier to use (for instance, the upside-down Ketchup bottle) or slightly improving a processor's performance. A more radical example is the introduction of new-to-the-world systems that greatly improve services, such as McDonald's recent adoption of digital kiosks that allow customers to visually choose their order without queuing up in front of the counter. This is akin to Schumpeter's "new products or services" typology.

– Process innovation is about "how we do it". This is what Schumpeter called "new methods of production". An incremental innovation of this kind could be the introduction of a new type of machine to speed up the production process. The use of assembly lines to manufacture high volumes of the original T Model car at low cost by Ford in the early 20th Century is an example of radical process innovation. "Conquering new sources of supply" is a Schumpeterian category that could also fit in this classification.

– Position innovation is about "who we target". Schumpeter referred to this as "opening up new markets". An incremental position innovation for a cosmetics company could consist of creating a new line of products positioned for older women or ethnic groups. A radical example would be targeting non-consumers, such as younger men.

– Paradigm innovation is about "changing the rules of the game" by combining product, service, position and process innovation in order to achieve what Schumpeter called "carrying out a new organization of an industry". It requires doing what Tidd and Bessant (2013) referred to as "new mental models" and often result in disruptive innovations, as described below.

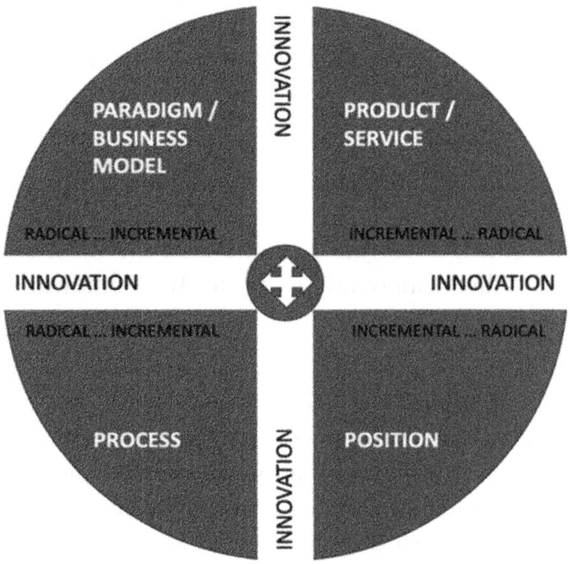

Figure 4.7. *Tidd and Bessant's innovation wheel (adapted from Tidd and Bessant 2013). For a color version of the figure, see http://www.iste.co.uk/lima/entrepreneurship.zip*

4.4.2. *Christensen's disruptive innovation*

Clayton Christensen (1997) introduced an important nuance in the traditional innovation typologies: according to him, more important than the degree of novelty of any given technology is the impact an innovation may have in the market. Sustaining innovations focus on addressing the needs and expectations of the most demanding (and often the most profitable) segments in the market. Disruptive innovations, on the contrary, often appear as inferior solutions that only appeal to fringe users due to its intrinsically different value proposition (typically lower cost or higher convenience). When these substitutes evolve on a steeper performance curve than the incumbent solution, however, disruptive innovations tend to displace incumbents by "changing the rules of the game", often creating whole new business models (Christensen *et al.* 2004).

A few examples of disruptive innovations include:

– **Digital photography**. The first digital camera was invented by Kodak in the 1970s. Because the company was run mostly by chemical engineers specialized in the properties of film, they could see no future in this expensive and cumbersome way of capturing images. Indeed, it was not until the advent of cellphones and miniaturized cameras that digital photography would take off. Very slowly, initially, the quality of the initial images was very poor and required perfect lighting conditions. However, this new solution to image capturing had two major advantages over film: they offered instant gratification and were easily shareable digitally. As smartphones became increasingly widespread, and computational photography became increasingly sophisticated, digital photography equaled and then surpassed the quality of film. Incapable of competing against this new trend, Kodak went bankrupt in the year.

– **Personal computers**. From the introduction of the transistor in the 1950s up until the early 1980s, so-called "mainframe" computers were the sole digital devices capable of storing and processing large datasets. In the late 1970s, Apple introduced the first widely adopted personal computer, the Apple II. One of the company founders (Steve Wozniak) managed to reconfigure low-cost chips in a very small board, creating a machine that could sell for a small fraction of the cost of a mainframe or minicomputer. Home users and offices could now afford to have a desktop solution that ran basic software like spreadsheets, word processors and data bases for a few hundred dollars where tens of thousands (or even hundreds of thousands of dollars) used to be required. Their initial capabilities would pale in comparison with professional mainframe systems. However, as personal computers became increasingly powerful and became networked to low-cost servers, they almost entirely replaced mainframes as the traditional computing platform.

– **Smartphones**. Up until the introduction of the iPhone in 2007, most web browsing was done in desktop computers or laptops. As the powerful combination of tactile screens, high processing power in your pocket and widespread Wi-Fi networks became available, people started shifting their navigation habits from PCs to their phones. Initially, surfing the web or using the phone as a laptop replacement to answer mails or write memos was awkward and slow. But as smartphone processors became faster and touch display technology became more efficient, people started switching several of their daily tasks to mobile systems. Most importantly, app ecosystems created opportunities for developers to reach hundreds of millions of people with innovative business models (free, fremium or subscription) that enabled billions of people to work and find entertainment anytime and anywhere. Smartphones are now the main computing platforms in several parts of the world.

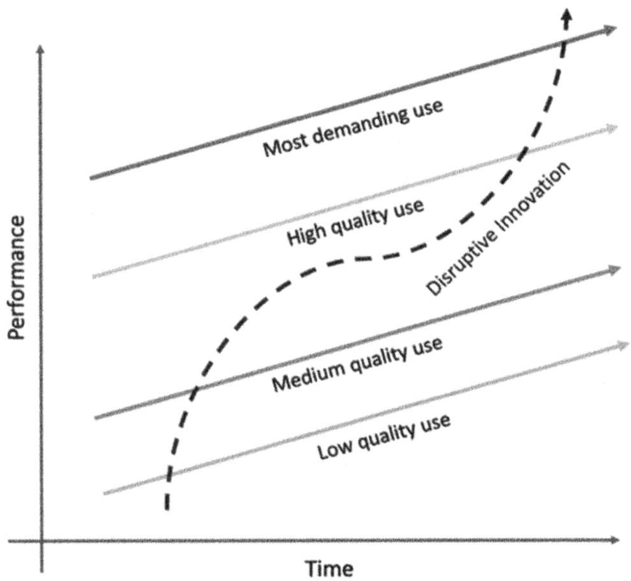

Figure 4.8. *Adoption rate of disruptive innovations (adapted from Christensen 1997). For a color version of the figure, see http://www.iste.co.uk/lima/entrepreneurship.zip*

These three examples have in common the fact that they all had very humble starts, while at the same time offering new benefits (lower cost, higher convenience) along a very steep growth curve. As Figure 4.8 illustrates, disruptive innovations start at a low performance level but take advantage of better technology or newer business models to overtake the low quality use of non-consumers at an early stage, then quickly moving towards medium- and high-quality levels until it is good enough to address the most demanding users, thus displacing incumbents who continue on their sustaining innovation trajectory.

Microsoft Office 365 is a good example of how, taken seriously, the concept of disruptive innovation can help innovative companies avoid obsolescence. In 2009, Google launched "Docs", an online suite of basic word processing, spreadsheets and presentation tools. Even if the original suite was very elementary compared to Microsoft's flagship product, the Redmond Giant did not underestimate the potential of this new rival to eventually dominate its market: being free (or freemium) and having very convenient distant collaboration tools, Google Docs was a credible alternative to basic users. In 2011, Microsoft launched Office 365, a freemium suite that would eventually cannibalize its traditional software packaging business model. Thanks to the willingness to change its innovation trajectory to catch up with the potentially disruptive trend of cloud-based applications, Microsoft remained a leader in this space. Cloud-driven solutions would become an integral part of Microsoft's innovation strategy. Thus, in 2014, the historical CEO Steve Ballmer stepped down to give the reins of the company to Satya Nadella, former vice president of the cloud division.

4.5. Visualizing business model innovation

The types of innovation discussed above can be visually represented with Osterwalder and Pigneur's BMC (2010). By visually depicting them, they illustrate how these innovations impact the nine building blocks differently.

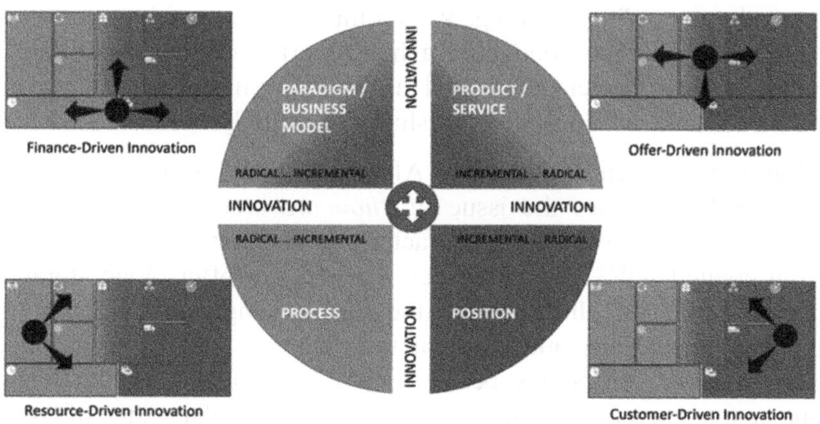

Figure 4.9. *Tidd's 4Ps (2013) associated with Osterwalder and Pigneur's (2010) innovation typology (compiled by the author). For a color version of the figure, see http://www.iste.co.uk/lima/entrepreneurship.zip*

According to Osterwalder and Pigneur, we can visualize four major "sources" of innovation using the Business Model Canvas:

– **Offer-driven innovation**. These are very similar to product/service innovation ("*what we sell*"). They involve changing the value proposition of the product/service offered and subsequently adapting the other elements of the canvas. By promising to deliver ready-made concrete on site for their construction customers in just four hours (compared to 48 hours for their competitors), Cemex became a worldwide leader in this industry. Such additional service performance, however, required rethinking their key activities (logistics), partnerships (data processing, platform development), key resources (data-driven expertise) in order to reduce costs and increase reliability. It also impacted channels (web-based and smartphone-based applications), created stronger customer relationship mechanisms (service platform) and increased revenues[2].

– **Customer-driven innovation**. Called "Position" innovation by Tidd and Bessant (2013), this type of innovation consists of rethinking the targeting strategy ("*whose needs we serve*") and repositioning the product accordingly. When creating the Wii gaming console, instead of targeting the same hard-core gamers as Microsoft's Xbox or Sony's Playstation, Nintendo decided to target non-gamers (young women, families, the elderly). Accordingly, they moved from a "more power for more sophisticated games" competition with the two main incumbents to a "less power, more user-friendly games" positioning. With a much more intuitive user interface and controls, Nintendo conquered a huge market of casual gaming, with much lower development costs and higher margins. They had to rethink distribution channels and key partnerships accordingly[3].

– **Resource-driven innovation**. Also known as "process" innovation, this approach addresses the issue of "*how we create value*". It requires rethinking the key resources, key activities and key partnerships. When Amazon created AWS (Amazon Web Services) to offer cloud storage and data management to third-parties, they were simply sharing with other companies the expertise and infrastructure that they had to put in place for their own needs. AWS has become more profitable than the historical e-commerce operation. More importantly, it transformed a source of costs into

2 Source: https://www.strategy-business.com/article/00325?gko=4acf9.

3 Source: https://hbr.org/2010/08/what-can-we-learn-from-ninten.

a very important source of revenue which continues to benefit all other Amazon divisions with its core competence[4].

– **Finance-driven innovation**. This final source of innovation is about redesigning "*how we make money*". It often requires rethinking the whole business from value creation to the value delivery process. Companies that have made a transition from products to service providers are a typical example of these so-called Product–Service Systems (Lima *et al.* 2019). Rolls-Royce, for instance, made a dramatic redesign of their business model, from merely selling airplane turbines, to also providing services around their "power by the hour" business model (a service package including the hardware, software and maintenance involved in using turbines).[5] Other typical finance-driven innovations include subscription services, leasing and pay-per-use models.

Osterwalder and Pigneur (2010) highlight that it is not always easy to locate the "epicenter" of the source of innovation, as there is a great interdependence between the components. A change in any of the building blocks requires rethinking the strategy for the others. A disruptive business model emerges when the combination of all of these types of innovation converges to create a much more cost-effective solution (initially with an inferior performance, but gradually catching up with incumbent solutions, as seen in Figure 4.8).

Table 4.2 lists dozens of business model innovation possibilities based on the four categories discussed. Note how in this list none of the business model types can be exclusively attributed to only one source of business model innovation. Most business model innovations require combining multiple dimensions of the BMC.

Main Source of BM Innovation	Business Model Templates
Offer-driven	information brokers, content provider, bundling, low touch, razors-and-blades, reverse razors-and-blades; product–service systems
Customer-driven	e-auction, third-party marketplace, direct to consumer, reverse auction
Resource-driven	e-procurement, value chain integrator, shared infrastructure, crowdsourcing
Finance-driven	advertising model, merchant model, manufacturer model, affiliate model, commission, subscription, crowdfunding, freemium, leasing, pay-as-you-go

Table 4.2. *Different business model templates categorized by the main source of innovation (adapted from Fielt 2014)*

4 Source: https://www.zdnet.com/article/in-2018-aws-delivered-most-of-amazons-operating-income/.

5 Source: https://knowledge.wharton.upenn.edu/article/power-by-the-hour-can-paying-only-for-performance-redefine-how-products-are-sold-and-serviced/.

4.6. Business modeling and the principle of effectuation

In Chapter 3, we presented a very structured template for analyzing the environment and planning for business development. Business planning is based on the principles of "causation", a belief that important events can and should be predicted in order to anticipate and prepare the best possible strategy, maximizing opportunities and minimizing threats.

This "causation" view of the entrepreneurial firm is being increasingly challenged by recent business thinkers (Dew *et al.* 2009; Chesbrough 2010). Saras Sarasvathy (2001) is the proponent of an opposite paradigm he called "effectuation". According to him, while causation takes effects as given and focuses on the means that will lead to those effects, "effectuation processes take a set of means as given and focus on selecting between possible effects that can be *created* with that set of means" (Sarasvathy 2001, p. 245). In other words, according to Sarasvathy, the underlying logic of causation is captured by the notion that "to the extent we can predict the future, we can control it" (i.e. by focusing on the predictable aspects of an uncertain future); conversely, in effectuation, the underlying rationale is "to the extent that we can control the future, *we do not need to predict it*" (rather, one should focus on the controllable elements). Innovators and entrepreneurs tend to thrive in ambiguity and are often exploiters of contingency rather than predicting analysts. According to Chesbrough (2010, p. 360),

> [entrepreneurs] do not analyze their environment so much as take actions that create new information that reveals latent possibilities in that environment. In other words, they do not study the market so much as enact it. There is a strong bias in effectuation for action over analysis, because there may be insufficient data available to analyze one's way towards a new business model: without action, no new data will be forthcoming.

Table 4.3, adapted from Dew *et al.* (2009), summarizes the differences between effectuation and causation.

Dimension (basis for decision-making)	Causation Paradigm	Effectuation Paradigm
View of the future	Predict the future	Create the future
Basis for taking action	Goal-oriented actions	Means-oriented actions
Attitudes towards the unexpected	Uncertainty avoidance	Leverage contingencies
View of risk and resources	Expected return mentality	Affordable loss mentality
Attitude towards outsiders	Competitive analysis	Partnership development

Table 4.3. *Principles of causation and effectuation paradigms (adapted from Dew* et al. *2009)*

The Society for Effectual Action has created a website (https://www.effectuation.org/) to summarize the five principles of effectuation mentioned above. They developed the following metaphors to illustrate them:

– **Pilot-in-the-plane principle** (create the future). An effectual worldview is based on the notion that the future is hardly predictable – but can be made. Part of the reason why certain individuals are attracted to entrepreneurship is the fact that they can forge their own future or pilot their own destiny. This belief often becomes a self-fulfilling prophecy among effectual entrepreneurs.

– **Bird-in-hand principle** (means-oriented action). Effectual entrepreneurs build new ventures with what they are, what they know and whom they know. They use their imagination to extrapolate what can be made with these resources (this principle is very similar to the visionary theory of Filion exposed in Chapter 2).

– **Lemonade principle** (leverage contingencies). Effectual entrepreneurs welcome the unexpected. Rather than exploring positive or negative scenarios, they take surprising elements ("lemons") as they appear and make the most of them ("lemonade").

– **Affordable loss principle** (how much can I invest rather than how much I expect to gain). Effectual venture creators limit risk by establishing small bets on unknown values rather than placing big bets on targets with high expected return over investment. This leads them to develop a trial-and-error approach to risk management that may lead either to unexplored opportunities or to very manageable, limited losses.

– **Crazy quilt principle** (partnership development). Effectual venture creators partner up with self-selecting stakeholders that help them co-create value. By obtaining their commitment early on, they establish an effective value chain to help develop the business opportunity. Rather than being obsessed by competitors and market analysis, their expanding network of partners determines the markets the company will enter or create.

The interaction of these five principles is illustrated in Figure 4.10. Everything starts with the entrepreneur's pilot-in-the-plane ambition to create their own future by starting a new business. If he or she is an effectual entrepreneur, he or she will start by the bird-in-hand questions: who am I, what do I know, who do I know? These questions will lead to the lemonade philosophy of determining "what can I do?" goals. But these goals will be constantly modified based on the crazy quilt principle of "who wants to join me?". Either the entrepreneur will be able to convince enough stakeholders surrounding stakeholders to commit resources to the new venture by using the "affordable loss" principle ("what have we got to lose?"), or the perceived risk or required resources will be too high (in which case the opportunity will remain on hold). If there is enough commitment and agreement among stakeholders, new means will be provided, and additional resources will be invested in new venture expansions, new products and new markets. If there is disagreement concerning the goals, new goals will be provided, and the process will be iterated with different constraints. Any changes in the environment will lead to adjustment and adaptation based on the new constraints and the new means available.

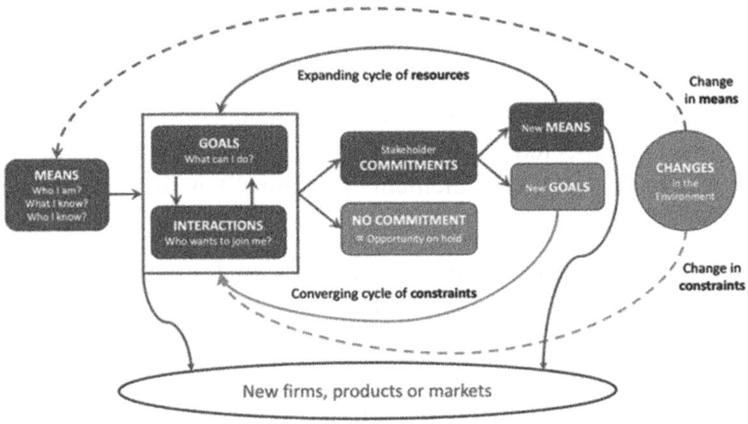

Figure 4.10. *The effectuation process (adapted from the Society for effectual Action, https://www.effectuation.org/). For a color version of the figure, see http://www.iste.co.uk/lima/entrepreneurship.zip*

4.7. Testing business model innovations

Business model design has been strongly influenced by the effectuation school of thought. Rather than taking for granted that our assumptions about trends, targets and value proposition are "correct", entrepreneurs should test these as if they were hypotheses and using the affordable loss principle. Small-scale experiments and preliminary real-world results can convince stakeholders that changes in the business model are feasible, desirable and marketable. Figure 4.11 presents these three perspectives for testing a business model:

– **From the resource perspective**, we must make sure the change is *feasible*. Do we have the required resources (human, technological, financial, material) to implement this innovation? Do we have the right competences to develop the necessary key activities? Have we found the right partners, which possess the resources and capabilities we lack?

– **From the customer perspective**, we must test the *desirability* of the potential innovation. Do the targeted segments really have an unmet need in this regard? Are they the right target at all? Desirable at what price? Through what channels?

– **From the finance perspective**, we must make sure the new business model is viable, that is, the cost of doing business will eventually become lower than the generated revenues. This is not a concern only regarding for-profit businesses: non-governmental organizations must also become financially sustainable if they are to be scaled up and have a larger impact.

A fourth source of hypotheses-to-be-tested is the external environment. As seen in Chapter 3, the entrepreneur must constantly scan the external environment for opportunities and threats in the PESTEL domains (political, economic, socio-cultural, ecological and legal), as well as among competitors. How adaptable is the business model if some of these opportunities or threats become unavoidable? To answer this question, one must go through the sources of business model innovation discussed above (offer-driven, customer-driven, resource-driven and finance-driven innovations) to check how to adjust to the new situation. It could also be a good idea to go through the 7S checklist (the integration between strategy, structure, systems, staff, style, skills and shared values), briefly discussed in Chapter 3 (and more deeply discussed in Chapter 6). Indeed, any change of strategy must be followed by an adaptation of the other organizational Ss involved.

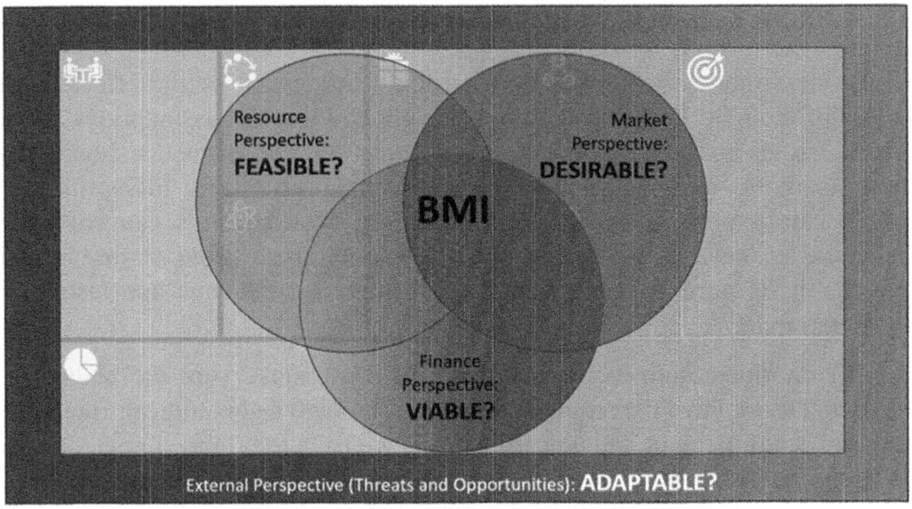

Figure 4.11. *Four key questions to ask about any innovation opportunity (adapted from Osterwalder 2016). For a color version of the figure, see http://www.iste.co.uk/lima/entrepreneurship.zip*

The so-called "ambidextrous" organizations (Tushman and O'Reilly 1996) are good at both exploiting current business models while exploring new ones. This organizational ambidexterity requires both causation and effectuation reasoning. On the one hand, organizations can use the known, predictable elements of the current business model to exploit incremental innovations in the current business model. On the other hand, they can explore and test new business models using the effectuation approach. This, according to Chesbrough (2010, p. 361), "demands leadership meta-skills in perceptions of the environment, in maintaining unity among the leadership team, and in the ability to reallocate resources to support new models".

The next chapter discusses how new products and services can be developed using both exploiting and exploring techniques.

4.8. Teaching business model innovation

In section 3.12 in Chapter 3, we suggested adopting individual projects that reflect the unique visionary process of each student. Apart from the peer review we built into that teaching approach, the initial draft of a business plan can be a very lonely journey. Not so with business modeling. As seen in this chapter, the canvas approach proposed by Osterwalder is inherently visual and collaborative. Therefore, emphasizing collaboration is paramount in the teaching techniques described below.

4.8.1. *Reflecting about the Business Model Canvas*

Before students can become autonomous in exploring the canvas, they must get deeply familiar with the framework. Osterwalder has published a series of six mini-videos (less than four minutes each) available on YouTube, telling the story of Beth and Carl, two young entrepreneurs who decide to quit their jobs and create an online travel agency for Baby Boomers.

In the first episode ("Getting from Business Idea to Business Model")[6], they present the characters and their idea. They highlight that most companies fail not necessarily because they have a poor idea for a product or a service, but because they did not develop the right business model to execute it appropriately. In the second episode ("Visualizing Your Business Model"), Beth and Carl illustrate the rationale behind the value flow in the Business Model Canvas. They achieve this by using the example of low-cost airlines. Episode three ("Prototyping") highlights the importance of trying out several different business model variations before settling in a more mature version of the initial idea. Episode four ("Navigating Your Environment") describes how external trends (market, competitors, economy, technology, etc.) affect business model development. In episode five ("Proving It"), we are reminded of the effectuation logic behind the BMC: all we have so far are hypotheses that need to be tested and validated in the real world. Finally, in the sixth episode, "Telling Your Story", Beth and Carl give several tips on how to present a BMC effectively.

This series of short videos can be enriched by all the frameworks exposed in this chapter. After episode 1, teachers can remind students that whereas the right side of the canvas is more related to marketing activities and the so-called "right side of the brain" (creativity, empathy, emotion), the operational left side is not less important. Indeed, the low-cost airline example illustrates how the left side can sometimes be more important than

6 Episode 1 available here: https://www.youtube.com/watch?v=wwShFsSFb-Y. The other five episodes are suggested in a chain starting from the first.

the right side. After the second episode, a discussion of Figures 4.1–4.6 can illustrate how value is created, delivered and captured in the canvas. Episode 4 is a good opportunity to remind students of the PESTEL+C framework discussed in Chapter 3. Episode 5 is the perfect spot to talk about effectuation (Figure 4.10) and the importance of constantly testing your assumptions when in unfamiliar territory, making sure your innovation is feasible, desirable and viable (Figure 4.11). The main takeaway of the final episode is that students should avoid overwhelming their audience by presenting all the visual information in a BMC at once (what they call "cognitive murder"). Instead, the value flow should be told like a story, starting on the right side with the value proposition and the customer segment and then slowly evolving towards the left side.

4.8.2. *Creating and authentic business model environment*

If teaching business models is to be a more collaborative process, then students should not necessarily use their own individual cases at first. Instead, we can have students discuss potential business model improvements for very innovative companies that they all admire (and are therefore fairly familiar with). Figure 4.12 presents a dashboard that teachers could use to assign students to their favorite firm (line 6).

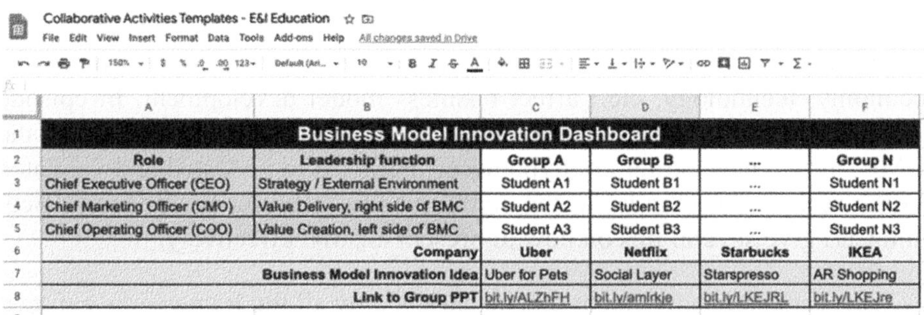

	A	B	C	D	E	F
1	Business Model Innovation Dashboard					
2	Role	Leadership function	Group A	Group B	...	Group N
3	Chief Executive Officer (CEO)	Strategy / External Environment	Student A1	Student B1	...	Student N1
4	Chief Marketing Officer (CMO)	Value Delivery, right side of BMC	Student A2	Student B2	...	Student N2
5	Chief Operating Officer (COO)	Value Creation, left side of BMC	Student A3	Student B3	...	Student N3
6		Company	Uber	Netflix	Starbucks	IKEA
7		Business Model Innovation Idea	Uber for Pets	Social Layer	Starspresso	AR Shopping
8		Link to Group PPT	bit.ly/ALZhFH	bit.ly/amlrkje	bit.ly/LKEJRL	bit.ly/LKEJre

Figure 4.12. *Collaborative dashboard to create multiple-role teams for innovation project (source: author). For a color version of the figure, see http://www.iste.co.uk/lima/entrepreneurship.zip*

To further increase this "authentic experience" feeling, teachers may create the opportunity for students to identify with different roles in the value creation chain. After deciding what kind of business model innovation they wish to pursue (see the examples in line 7 in Figure 4.12), they can divide the work of preparing their final presentation and report. A "Chief Executive Officer (CEO)" can take a leadership role in researching the external environment to understand the opportunities and threats surrounding the idea. They can specialize in the process of using databases to better understand customer segments, competitors, technological trends, etc. Another student can take the role of "Chief Marketing Officer (CMO)", specializing in the right side of the BMC (value delivery). This student can research the Web to understand the current value delivery system of this company and the business model components that will be affected by the proposed idea. Finally, a "Chief Operating Officer" would specialize in adapting the value creation side of the BMC to the new idea, identifying the key resources, activities and partners for the new project, as well as the key cost components of the new venture.

By researching the existing business model of companies which they admire, students should be in a better position to propose an innovation strategy to further develop their products and services. After this experience, they should be capable of better reflecting about their own entrepreneurial projects.

4.8.3. *Using technology to make it more interactive and collaborative*

There are a number of "freemium" online collaboration tools that facilitate business model design[7]. However, most of them have a limited number of free features that are designed to push the user to sign up for a paying account. For this reason, we suggest students use collaborative tools like Google Slides or Microsoft 365, depending on which platform is readily available in their school.

Each group should create one shared document "on the cloud" and paste the link in the collaborative dashboard (see line 8 in Figure 4.12). They should configure the link as "anyone with access to this link may edit it". Thus, not only can other team members work anywhere anytime on the

7 For instance, Conceptboard.com (https://conceptboard.com/blog/business-model-canvas/) and Visual-paradigm.com (https://www.visual-paradigm.com/features/business-model-canvas-tool/).

development of the canvas, but other students and the teacher can also access it and make suggestions.

It is important to remind students of a few rules to make the most of this collaborative environment:

– **They must respect each other's work**. As we previously mentioned, with the power of editing each other's documents comes the responsibility to use this power wisely. Any breach of trust should lead to making these links private and requiring nominal login to avoid vandalism, which would considerably impoverish the collaborative experience.

– **They should be encouraged to visit links by other groups and be inspired by their progress**. Part of the wealth of this project-based learning is the ability to compare group outputs. If one group is stuck trying to define their value proposition, they should look at how other groups have approached the problem. Because each project is unique, there is no danger of "copying and pasting" each other's work.

– **Everyone must work**. By creating "specialization roles", we have clearly defined who should lead each stage of the project development. Besides the empowerment that goes with role playing, this approach has the additional benefit of identifying who's working on which aspects of the problem. During partial presentations with randomly selected groups throughout the semester, the teacher can clearly identify if one of the "leaders" is not doing their part to help the group Excel and take appropriate measures to "encourage" laggards (suggesting differentiated grading or having a face-to-face talk with unmotivated students, for example).

Now that students know how to design their business model, it is time to enter the product development stage. The following chapter proposes a few tools and approaches to that part of the innovation and entrepreneurship journey.

5

From Business Model Design to Design Thinking and Lean Startup

"Build it and they will come"
is not a strategy; it's a prayer.

Steve Blank,
The Four Steps to the Epiphany

Innovation has been defined as "a good idea well executed" (Brown and Katz 2019). So far, we have discussed the former and not the latter part of the innovation process. In the three preceding chapters, we have seen how to develop one's idea from an emergent to a more mature vision. But having a clear vision is not enough. Success depends much more on the way it is executed. This is the product development part of innovation. The rather static exercise of business planning and the more dynamic exercise of business modeling are a necessary prelude to this phase. Now, we must start discussing how to go from ideas to market.

We will start with the traditional way companies have developed products for the past 70 years, the so-called "stage-gate" approach. This is clearly based on the causation rationale previously presented. We will then discuss the more recent influences of agile project management and effectuation on a fairly recent approach known as "Design Thinking".

5.1. New product development: the traditional stage-gate approach

The process of structuring investment decisions in phases has been used in large projects throughout the second half of the 20th Century. Large companies or complex organizations like NASA pioneered the notion of reducing risk by establishing a number of criteria that projects must meet (known as "kill gates") before proceeding from one stage to the next. Robert Cooper (1990) systematized the methodology known as stage-gate, as illustrated in Figure 5.1.

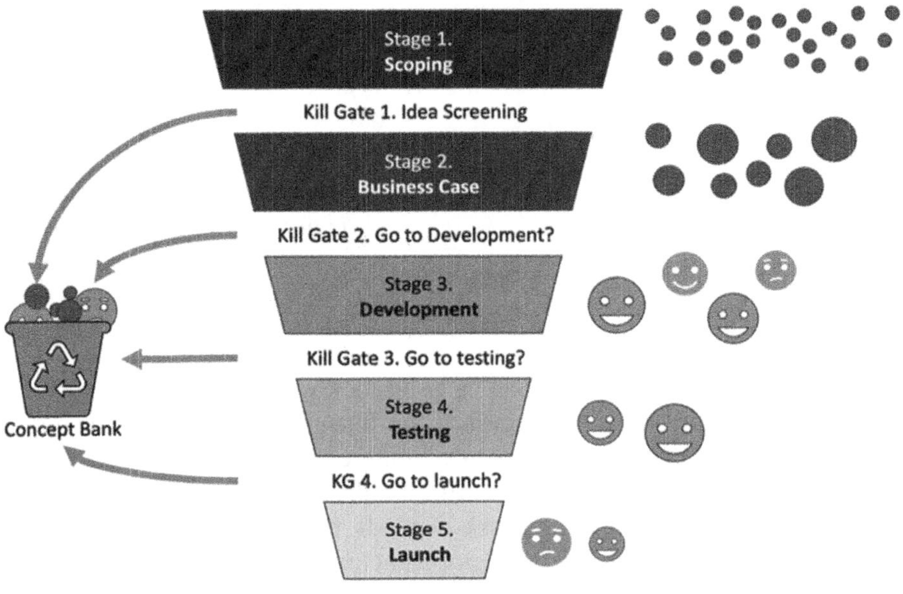

Figure 5.1. *The stage-gate system (adapted from Cooper 1990). For a color version of the figure, see http://www.iste.co.uk/lima/entrepreneurship.zip*

In stage 1 (Scoping), intrapreneurs or entrepreneurs must scan the environment in search of opportunities for new products, services or business model innovation. These opportunities must be screened according to the criteria presented in Figure 4.11 (four key questions to ask about any innovation opportunity), such as: Is the opportunity technologically feasible? Is it desirable by our current and potential customers? Is it viable/profitable? Can we adapt our business model to explore this new opportunity? The priority here is to assess market size, potential and product acceptance, as well as preliminary technical feasibility and execution costs. It could be a good idea to list all the customer needs that are currently not being addressed (or poorly addressed) by existing solutions.

Opportunities that survive stage 1 will benefit from a larger financial commitment at stage 2 (Business Case). Similar feasibility, desirability and viability questions will be asked at this stage, but a business case must be established with precise figures and projections. Cooper (1990) recommends that this more in-depth assessment should involve a literature review using market databases and statistics, contact with lead users, focus groups and testing the concept with potential adopters. Reliable financial projections are also required. A market analysis with additional information about market size, segmentation, growth, customer behavior and channel strategy must be discussed. Early prototypes can be target segments for qualitative feedback. The go/no-go decision at this stage is critical, as it is the last stage before the very expensive product development phase. A very clear product definition is the expected output at this stage.

At stage 3 (Development), detailed manufacturing, distribution and marketing plans must be developed in detail. Legal consultation about patent/copyright issues must be addressed. Safety, health and environmental compliance are also determined. This stage revisits the three key questions of feasibility, desirability and viability in greater detail with more reliable data, and pre-commercialization decisions are made. A project plan must be elaborated to determine a clear road map for the final stages (with estimated cost and time to market). Milestones of the project must follow the SMART principles: they must be specific, measurable, actionable, realistic and timely. The main deliverable of this stage is a final prototype which should go extensive testing and assessment in the next phase.

The final two stages are testing and launching. They involve in-house testing of products to check quality and performance, user trials to verify compliance with expectations and real-world conditions, pilot production processes to determine precise production costs and yield rates, and pretest in a pilot market to measure the effectiveness of the launch plan, with expected market share and revenues. After the launch, a post-implementation review must be conducted to compare actual and forecast data on revenues, expenditures, profits and timing. This is also the moment when a critical assessment of the project's positive and negative feedback may lead to organizational learning and improvement for future innovation projects.

Sales teams must be prepared for the launch, and the marketing strategy must be shared with all the stakeholders involved.

It is important to note that not all projects are subjected to the same degree of rigor and scrutiny. Smaller and less risky projects do not necessarily have to go through all the stages and gates or may do so more quickly. For several decades, this process or slight variations of it have provided innovators with a roadmap to facilitate decision-making, objectives and task definition. It has the merit of rendering explicit the risks involved at each stage, forcing project team members to think deeply before committing more company resources.

In spite of its pioneering benefits, however, the stage-gate process has faced an increasing wave of criticisms. Some authors argue that the original process does not involve partners and other stakeholders (Grönlund *et al.* 2010). Others argue that the process often lacks agility, taking too long to make critical decisions in a fast-paced competitive environment (Sommer *et al.* 2015).

Indeed, the original stage-gate process is part of what might be called a "closed innovation system". In this model, both product development and marketing take place within the firm, with little or no input from partners and customers. Henry Chesbrough (2003) coined the term "open innovation" to refer to an approach "that assumes that firms can and should use external ideas as well as internal ideas, and internal and external paths to market, as the firms look to advance their technology" (Chesbrough 2003, p. xxiv). Those external sources of ideas could involve not only suppliers and competitors but also communities of consumers, what may be termed as co-creation or crowdsourcing of solutions. Even though external collaboration has arguably always existed in the history of innovation, the information age has enabled new mechanisms of collaboration that create new opportunities to identify and co-exploit value creation processes.

Grönlund *et al.* (2010) suggest that the original stage-gate approach could benefit from the insights of open innovation during the design and validation stages. Inbound open innovation activities that could enrich the original approach include acquiring or licensing solutions from suppliers, competitors or firms in analogous markets. Conversely, for ideas that have been rejected or thrown into the "concept bank", outbound open innovation activities should be considered, such as out-licensing or selling patents to suppliers, competitors or firms in other markets which may be better positioned to develop them.

Robert Cooper has recently updated his model (2014) to make it nimbler and faster in an age of very quick product development. Sommer *et al.* (2015) built on these ideas to propose what they call "agile stage-gate" based on Scrum techniques for project management. Originally applied in the software industry, Scrum uses a product backlog of ideas and features to be added to an existing or new product, based on customer expectations and needs. These features must be developed in very short bursts of collaborative work known as "sprints", which typically last between two and four weeks. During a sprint, 15-minute daily meetings are held in front of a white board filled with sticky notes representing the current state of development. After each sprint, the new features are tested and fed back into the product backlog for re-evaluation/re-prioritization. Sommer *et al.* (2015) argue that adding this iterative layer to every phase of the stage-gate approach creates a more agile, faster version of Cooper's original framework.

However, neither open innovation nor agile adaptations of the stage-gate process address the fact that it remains a very technology-push-centric approach. Furthermore, it often assumes "an established, well-defined market where the basis of competition is understood, and its customers are known" (Blank 2020, p. 2). Steven Blank, one of the pioneers of the Lean Startup approach, argues that few entrepreneurs have the luxury of as many certainties. Therefore, according to this new school of thought, traditional product development frameworks are inadequate for startups. In the following section, we discuss how alternative frameworks for iterative product development are influencing innovation management by increasing the amount of empathy with unmet customer needs at every stage, thus creating a better balance between technology push and market pull throughout the process. These new methods are being used not only by startups but increasingly by intrapreneurs in large firms dealing with very high levels of uncertainty.

5.2. Customer development

According to Steven Blank (2020, p. 6), the traditional product development model exposed above ignores the fact that

> the greatest risk – and hence the greatest cause of failure – in startups is not in the development of the new product but in the

> development of customers and markets. Startups don't fail because they lack a product; they fail because they lack customers and a proven financial model.

Companies often focus on the ship date of a new product and work backwards through the product development project to make sure that everything will be ready by that deadline. He argues that startups must do the opposite: develop customers before they develop products. Focus on learning and discovery by experimentation rather than execution. Before planning any product development steps, a startup team must answer key questions such as, "How well do I understand my customer's problems, pains and expectations? Will our product address those unmet needs?" This manifesto, known as Customer Development, was originally published in 2003 and is one of the main sources of the Lean Startup movement created by Blank's disciple, Eric Ries. Alex Osterwalder's Business Model Canvas is considered by Blank as a "front end" to organize the Customer Development hypotheses.

This iterative effectuation movement is quite critical of relying on business plan tools such as the ones presented in Chapter 3. Their proponents believe that it does not make sense to position, segment, target and market products before the first sales have been made. Blank (2020) calls this the "marketing death march", leading to premature scaling of operations before all business model premises have been tested and validated. On the contrary, they argue, it is initial sales that should iteratively determine how to position a product, who to target and how to market it. This model was created because "while educators and startup investors had adapted tools and processes useful for *executing* a business model, there were no tools and processes to *search* for a business model" (Blank 2020, p. ix). Figure 5.2 illustrates the difference between the search and execution processes.

Customer Development is by no means a replacement for a Product Development process, but a necessary addition to it. In startups, Customer Development should run in parallel to Product Development (particularly the kind of iterative, empathetic product development process called "Design Thinking", which we will discuss in the next section). The recursive arrows in each step of this model are the main philosophical difference with the principles of a linear Product Development funnel. These arrows suggest a test-and-validate approach throughout the process; nothing is taken for granted until tested.

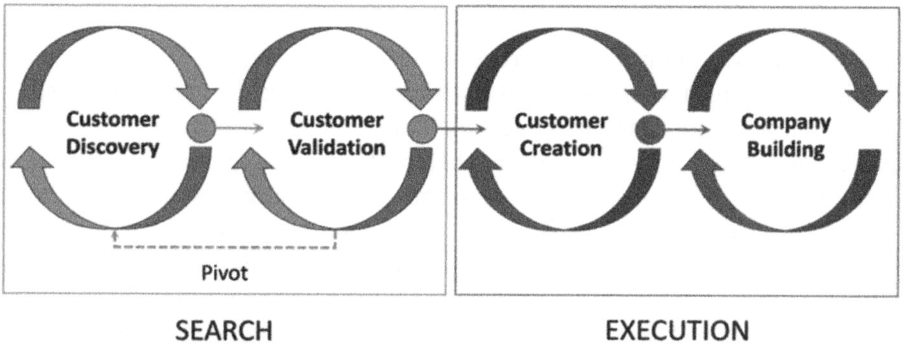

Figure 5.2. *The Customer Development Model (Blank 2020). For a color version of the figure, see http://www.iste.co.uk/lima/entrepreneurship.zip*

Customer Discovery is the process of testing if a company's business model has potential. This cannot be done in the comfort of an armchair; one must go to the field and learn first-hand from real customers whether one's business model hypotheses are correct. This is an iterative look for the perfect fit between value proposition and target segments. In this process, it is crucial to identify what Blank calls "earlyvangelists" – customers willing to take a risk on a product that is still in early stages of development. Nowadays, this is easily done by creating a crowdfunding campaign on platforms like Kickstarter or Indiegogo. Instead of developing a product for a mass market with a large number of product features, Customer Discovery involves finding a few customers who are naturally aligned with the original vision and focus on solving their problem in the best possible way. This will be the time to validate hypotheses about what the problem is and how it can best be solved from the earlyvangelists' perspective.

Customer Validation is the process of developing a scalable sales model. "Earlyvangelists" may turn out to be too few to justify creating a sustainable business. Scalability can only be achieved by successfully selling early versions of the products to a larger group of customers. Instead of spending time and money into developing a product only a few enthusiasts may want, this stage makes sure that a large enough number of customers are willing to pay for a minimum viable product. This stage should help refine ideas about segment attractivity, product differentiating features, adapted channels and pricing decisions. Typical questions at this stage are: Do we have a product/market fit? Do we understand the sales process? Are the product and the company correctly positioned? Is our profit equation sound?

Customer Creation is the process of driving end-user demand using classic marketing tools. Now that assumptions about the value proposition and the target market are validated, it is time to spend heavily in driving a demand we now know does exist. Different market types require different Customer Creation strategies: if entering a new market with an unknown product, for instance, startups need to spend a considerable amount of resources educating customers about product benefits and how to use it. This will take considerably more time and money than entering an existing market with a well-known product category. In this latter case, the effort will be to emphasize the differentiating attributes of the new product (lower cost, higher convenience, etc.). This is the stage when certain digital strategies known as "Growth Hacking" may come in handy: large-scale, low-cost solutions to reaching large audiences by using social media, viral marketing, email marketing, search engine optimization, web analytics, content marketing, inbound marketing, etc. (Holiday 2014).

Company Building is the process of transitioning an organization from learning and discovery mode to an execution machine. This is when startups can finally ramp up their production, as they have clear evidence that their business model is well adjusted and scalable. It must transform itself from an *ad hoc* team of polyfunctional founders into an agile and nimble but more formally structured organization.

Blank's greatest insight was that customers must be discovered and validated before products can be developed. This insight was deepened by two parallel movements that were taking place in the early 2000s: Design Thinking and Lean Startup. In order to understand how these converging ideas emphasize different aspects of the same phenomenon, it is useful to observe the visual synthesis proposed by Brand *et al.* (2019) of Gartner, Inc. in Figure 5.3.

The "Customer Problem" and "Customer Solution" phases in this diagram are very reminiscent of the "Customer Discovery" and "Customer Validation" stages in Blank's pioneer work (which precede the execution stages of "Customer Creation" and "Company Building"). In the first stage, entrepreneurs must identify unmet needs in an existing solution. This can be done partly by researching secondary data (surveys, databases, official statistics), but most useful insights will derive from talking to real customers to understand their pain points and, above all, to observe them. The insights gained in this phase must be systematized and discussed in groups before a concrete innovation problem can be framed. This is followed by the prototyping stage (build/measure/learn). The data generated in this iterative, agile process may lead either to the validation of the solution or to a pivot of the original idea, which would then require going back to another cycle of design thinking ideation. If the agile iteration results in a proven product that customers are ready to pay for, then the execution stage of scaling up may take place. This is the stage when certain aggressive marketing practices known as "Growth Hacking" may be applied.

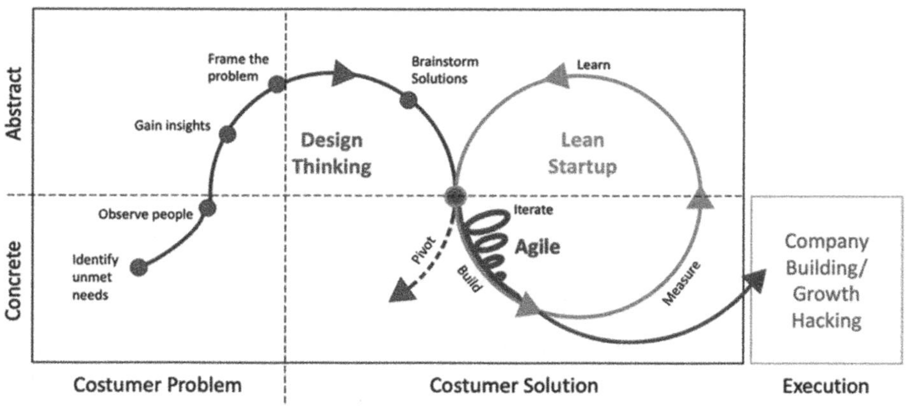

Figure 5.3. *Design Thinking and Lean Startup approaches to innovation (adapted from Brand* et al. *2019). For a color version of the figure, see http://www.iste.co.uk/lima/entrepreneurship.zip*

Some critics (Appelo 2020) argue that these cycles should not be presented in a linear succession, as if Design Thinking were a prerequisite for Lean Startup or Agile Development to finally culminate with Growth Hacking. Instead, they see these cycles as variations on the same theme of "continuous improvement". Indeed, Design Thinking was created by and for designers, who are more focused on the early stages of product development. Lean Startup was created by and for startuppers, who can afford to build "crazy" prototypes and see which of them gain most market traction without jeopardizing their reputation or market status. Agile development appeared first among coders who understood that all product features do not have equal priorities; therefore, they should validate high-priority features before they commit to low-priority ones. In a sense, all of these are versions of the basic principle of iterative discovery, delivery and improvement.

Nonetheless, because they were created by different types of product developers with different biases, these variations on the same theme do have noteworthy differences. In order to make this case, the following sections will analyze more in depth the stages involved in Design Thinking and Lean Startup. A briefer commentary on Agile Development and Growth Hacking will be added in the third section, before discussing approaches to teaching these concepts.

5.3. Design thinking

Design Thinking is not so much a methodology as it is a set of generic principles. It is a "philosophy of empathy" that may be translated by the three "spaces of innovation" proposed by Tim Brown: "inspiration, ideation, implementation". Brown is the Executive Chair of IDEO and one of the early proponents of this approach. IDEO, one of the world's most prestigious design firms, was founded by David Kelley. Design Thinking cases became one of the pillars of the Design School of Stanford (Hasso Plattner Institute of Design, simply known as d.school), founded by Kelley. Design Thinking principles have since irrigated Silicon Valley, followed by the whole planet, with a novel approach to product development.

In their book "Change by Design" (revised in 2019, 10 years after its first publication), Brown and Katz argue that "the mission of design thinking is to translate observations into insights and insights into products and services that will improve lives" (page 55). This is achieved largely through the capacity of designers to empathize with user feelings and emotions, not just with the functional specifications of design solutions.

Before Design Thinking influenced product development and innovation, it was common practice to trust the instincts of engineers in deciding which product features should be kept or eliminated in a stage-gate-like process (see above). The problem with this approach is that product managers seldom have the ability to understand problems from the perspective of users and clients. Relying on customer surveys and focus groups can be equally dangerous, as there is a remarkable gap between what people say and how they truly feel.

Figure 5.4 illustrates this "armchair decision-making" problem. Ideas with innovation potential come from either learning-by-doing processes (also called learning by exploiting what is already known) or learning-by-searching processes (also called learning by exploring or simply research and development). How many of these ideas will become innovation projects depends on the "filters" the organization puts in place to select "good" ideas from "bad" ones (institutional barriers and incentives, a3 and b3). These barriers are impregnated with the perceptions of decision-makers, who are often managers and engineers far removed from the day-to-day use of their products and services.

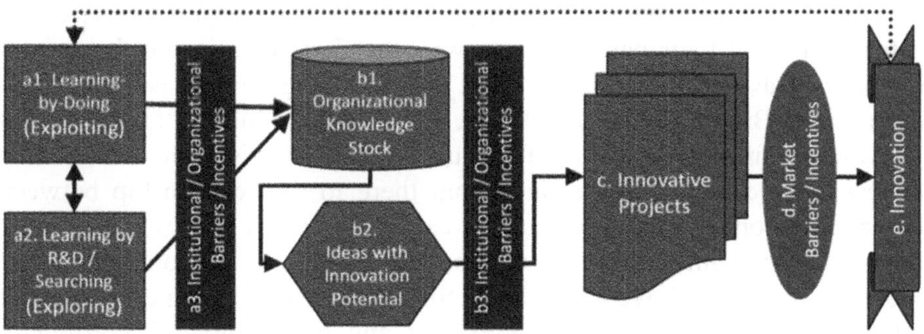

Figure 5.4. *Traditional organizational learning and innovation (based on Lima 1997). For a color version of the figure, see http://www.iste.co.uk/lima/entrepreneurship.zip*

A Design Thinking organization would look more like Figure 5.5. Instead of trusting "enlightened geniuses" to decide which ideas should be promoted or demoted, designers prefer to use iterative processes of learning from the "real world" (market stakeholders, lead users, expert customers). This iterative process requires ideas to be tested as early as possible in order to "fail often in order to succeed sooner", as one of the IDEO's mottos suggests.

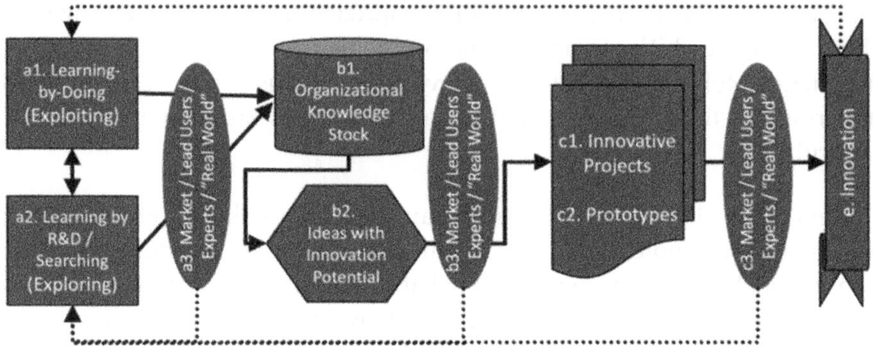

Figure 5.5. *Learning in an organization embedded with DT principles. For a color version of the figure, see http://www.iste.co.uk/lima/entrepreneurship.zip*

The job of the people involved in this iterative, on-going process is, as Peter Drucker once said, "to convert need into demand". But understanding unmet needs requires the ability to immerse oneself in the perspective of the customer, to feel their pains. This is why the first stage in the framework created by David Kelley's d.school at Stanford (Figure 5.6) is "empathy". According to Brown and Katz (2019, p. 47), Design Thinking "is the story of the evolution from the creation of products to the analysis of the relationship between people and products, and from there to the relationship between people and people.' This is what they call "user-centric design". The main question at this initial stage is to find out "what is" not only by using secondary data, but above all by collecting primary data using ethnographic methods such as interviews with experts and observation. According to Brown, this is stage is about "watching what people don't do, listening to what they don't say".

The second stage is about defining the problem or unmet needs. This can be done with the assistance of a technique called Customer Journey Mapping (Knap *et al.* 2016, see section 5.5 for details, below). A CJM helps visualize the main pain points, frustrations and frictions perceived by users trying to extract value from their experience with the existing solution. This is not just about expected function, but also about the emotional journey of the customer. Together with "empathize", this stage helps define *what is* the problem and the related *unmet needs*.

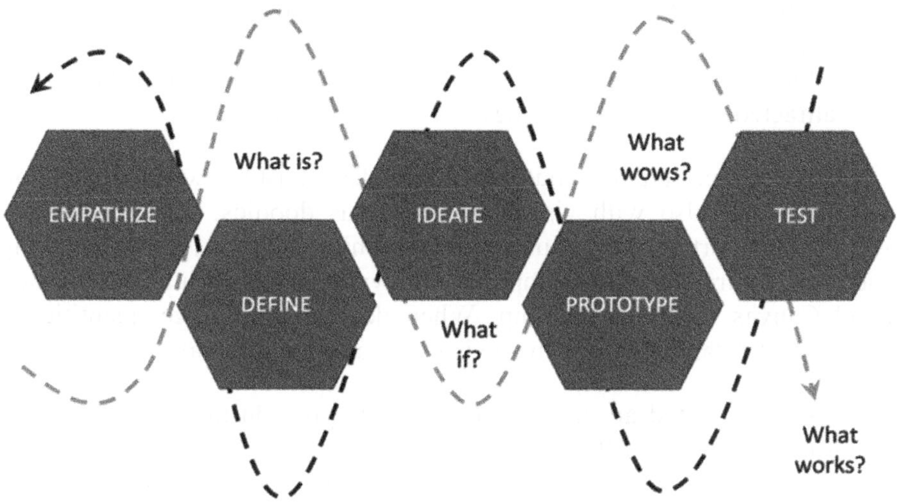

Figure 5.6. *Design Thinking stages (adapted from the d.school framework, Stanford). For a color version of the figure, see http://www.iste.co.uk/lima/entrepreneurship.zip*

The next stage is ideation. According to Brown and Katz (2019), it is important to establish clear rules to extract the best of group ideas without falling prey to homogeneous group thinking. In his words (p. 84), "at IDEO we have dedicated rooms for our brainstorming sessions, and the rules are literally written on the walls: 'Defer judgment. Encourage wild ideas. Stay focused on the topic.' The most important of them, I would argue, is 'Build on the ideas of others.'" This stage is characterized by the overall question "what if?". It marks the transition from divergent thinking (more and more ideas are created and posted on the walls as sticky notes, doodles and photographs) to convergent thinking (focusing on the most promising ideas found). To facilitate convergence, IDEO uses a technique known as the "butterfly test", invented by Bill Moggridge (co-founder of the company). It is, according to Brown and Katz (2019, p. 89),

> "a thoroughly unscientific but amazingly effective process for extracting a few key insights from a mass of data". Let's imagine that by the end of a deep research phase, numerous brainstorming sessions, and endless prototypes, an entire wall of the project room has been covered with promising ideas. Each participant is then given a small number of small Post-it

> "ballots" to attach to the ideas they think should move forward. Members of the team flutter about the room inspecting the tableau of ideas, and before long it is clear which ones have attracted the most "butterflies".

In order to facilitate this "butterfly test", ideas must be expressed not only with words but also with visual tools such as doodles, story boards and icons. This is part of the "visual thinking" philosophy of Design Thinking, which has inspired other contemporary innovation tools such as the Business Model Canvas and Lean Startup. When dealing with large quantities of ill-structured data, often "one image is worth a thousand words".

The ideas selected are then built into prototypes during the fourth stage and tested during the fifth. This is the moment to deliver something that wows (emotional/social needs) and something that works (functional needs). Prototyping and testing help to determine what is feasible, desirable and economically viable, thus fulfilling the main criteria of an innovation as we saw in the previous chapter. The main idea at these final stages, which will be further developed in the Lean Startup movement, is that you cannot get customer feedback abstractly. You need to test a concrete artifact in the real world to make sure it lives up to their expectations in every detail. This is not done by spending months developing a final product, but a couple of days (sometimes a few hours!) creating a "low-resolution" version of the object or experience. This is what David Kelley called to "think with your hands".

Prototyping and testing are not something that only startups should do. Brown and Katz (2019, pp. 113–114) narrate the following case to illustrate how multinationals are increasingly adopting Design Thinking principles:

> McDonald's is a company famous for applying the prototyping process throughout each of the spaces of innovation. In the inspirational space, designers use sketches, quick mock-ups, and scenarios to explore new services, product offerings, and customer experiences. These might be kept under wraps or shown to management or consumers to get early feedback. To nurture the ideation space, McDonald's has built a sophisticated prototyping facility at its headquarters outside Chicago where project teams can configure every type of cooking equipment, point-of-sale technology, and restaurant layout to test new ideas.

> When a new idea is almost ready for implementation, it will often be tested in the form of a pilot deployed at selected restaurants.

One of the major service innovations that resulted from this process was the self-ordering kiosks[1]. This shift in user experience (UX) design was initially extensively prototyped before being pilot tested in a few stores and finally generalized in 2015. The prototype helped establish the best user interface design for the kiosk and make design decisions that would impact cost, convenience and effectiveness.

Large companies are increasingly adopting DT approaches to innovation. Appendix D details the results of a survey we have conducted with 105 French and Russian businesses about the adoption of the DT tools and their perceived effectiveness[2]. It shows that the most important perceived barriers to DT adoption are lack of skills and organizational culture and structure. Chapter 8 will discuss in detail how knowledge management best practices can minimize these barriers.

5.4. Lean startup

Eric Ries was a devout student under Steve Blank at the University of California at Berkley in the early 2000s. The ideas in the Customer Development manifesto of his mentor were refined by Ries (2011) in the framework that came to be known as "Lean Startup", which gained momentum in the last decade alongside with other iterative approaches such as the Business Model Canvas and Design Thinking. This method can be summarized in Figure 5.7.

Lean Startup derives its name and several of its influences from the Lean Manufacturing movement in the Japanese automobile industry during the 20th Century. The underlying principle behind the "lean" moniker is this: everything that does not create value must be considered waste. Therefore, focus *only* on value creating activities, discarding all others.

---

1 https://uxplanet.org/service-design-the-case-of-mcdonalds-196ac9d5d7f0.

2 This was part of a research project in association with Anna Komarova of the Franco-Russian University initiative. As part of this project, Skema Business School partnered with the Russian Foreign Trade Academy to investigate the use of Design Thinking in France and Russia (Kamarova and Lima 2020).

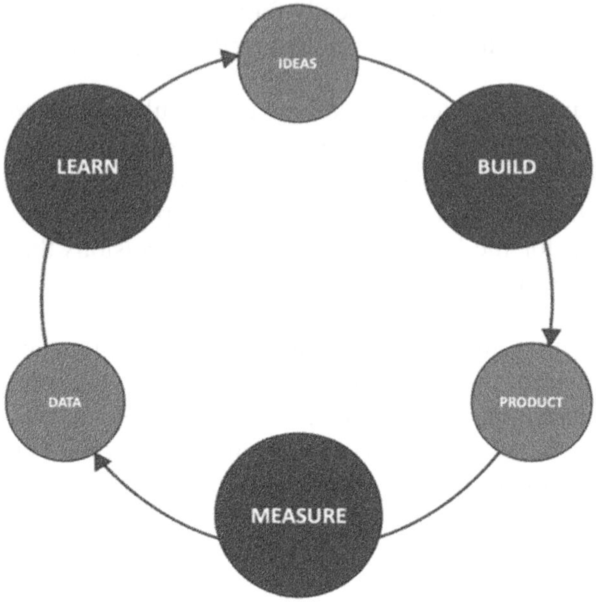

Figure 5.7. *Lean Startup cycle (Ries, 2011). For a color version of the figure, see http://www.iste.co.uk/lima/entrepreneurship.zip*

When applied to startups and product development processes, this principle yields the following premises:

– Products should not be developed until hypotheses about its desirability are proven; therefore, instead of spending resources planning product development stages, startups should create a **Minimum Viable Product** (MVP) that must be tested with actual consumers before further development.

– Entrepreneurs should share the skepticism of scientists who never assume something to be true until measurable hypotheses have been formulated and tested using experiments. Therefore, product development decisions should be based on **actionable metrics**, data that reflects the value creation process. It is important to measure what really matters and avoid "vanity metrics" (i.e. metrics which, while reassuring, do not create real value for the company and the customer).

– Startups must remain flexible and change their business model as soon as validated learning (hypotheses confirmation) indicates that their current value creation process is not sustainable. This is called *pivoting*. Changing course is an opportunity to establish new ideas, leading to building a better minimum viable product in order to measure its value creation potential. This new MVP will yield data, leading to validated learning opportunities that will help refine the idea.

Every Lean Startup process must be controlled by what Ries calls "innovation accounting": measuring progress by setting up experiments, milestones, prioritizing tasks and establishing accountability for every key project. This should not keep entrepreneurs from thinking big, but it definitely means they should start small and build their value system gradually, iteratively.

It may be argued that Lean Startup principles are best applicable in industries with rapid iteration product development cycles, such as software and information technology solutions. Some of the principles, such as continuous deployment (code modules for an application are released continuously, as soon as it is written) and A/B testing (comparing data from two different versions of a user interface or application), were clearly drawn from Ries' background as an application developer.

As shown in Figure 5.7, above, Lean Startup may be considered as a zoom into the prototyping and testing stages of Design Thinking. It assumes an agile organization, capable of pivoting fast and adapting its strategy and structure according to the constraints of an extremely uncertain environment. We will discuss more about adaptable organizations in Chapter 6.

In summary, we can argue that Lean Startup focuses on the customer discovery and business model validation stages of Steve Blank's Customer Development process seen earlier in this chapter. Only once demand is clearly validated through this approach can a startup begin to scale up. This final execution stage, called "company building" by Blank, can be boosted by aggressive marketing techniques such as Growth Hacking.

Defined by Sean Ellis in a blog post in 2010[3] as a decision-maker obsessed with growth metrics, a Growth Hacker uses a data-driven approach to every marketing decision concerning customer service, product positioning and feature development. These approaches include

3 https://www.startup-marketing.com/where-are-all-the-growth-hackers/.

understanding customer sentiment through online interaction (social listening), developing omnichannel presence, optimizing search engine results, creating viral content, boosting inbound traffic, using social media dashboards to monitor online presence and creating loyalty and prescription programs to retain current users and conquer new ones.

It might be argued that Growth Hacking is just a catch phrase for using digital marketing tools aggressively to scale up a business with a validated value proposition. This is one of the crucial insights from the Lean Startup framework. You should not start the process of "Growth Hacking" (i.e. spending precious resources on scaling up) as long as the startup stage has not been validated with clear metrics. Many startups go bankrupt for failing to understand this notion. It is pointless to try to gain traction with a product nobody wants using scarce resources that may be best deployed at a later stage of the business cycle. Therefore, Growth Hacking and Company Building can only happen after the Design Thinking and Lean Startup exercises have been fully developed to make sure your prototype of product or service fulfills an unmet need.

5.5. Teaching Design Thinking and Lean Startup

As previously mentioned, Design Thinking and Lean Startup are often perceived as vague conceptual principles that advocate iterative short cycles of empathizing, prototyping and testing. When teaching these principles using project-based pedagogy, we do need a solid, simple step-by-step framework to guide students in their learning path. Jake Knapp provides us with just what we need in his best-selling book *Sprint: How to Solve Big Problems and Test New Ideas in Just Five Days* (Knapp *et al.* 2016)[4].

Knapp and his colleagues created a process of validated learning, which is called "Design Sprint", by adapting the principles of Design Thinking and Lean Startup to a very short and fast cycle of just five days. Inspired from their experience with agile software development methods, this tool was used at Google Ventures to decide which projects they should fund. They

4 Knapp started his career as a designer at Google in 2007. In 2012, he joined Google Ventures (GV). After leaving GV, he spent two years as a "visiting fellow designer" at IDEO, where his insights about accelerating the Design Thinking process through short "sprints" were highly appreciated.

worked with very successful entrepreneurs to develop this method, like Ev Williams (creator of Twitter, Blogger and Medium) and Chad Hurley and Steve Chen (founders of YouTube). Knapp's most important contribution was to condense the whole process in an intensive and "sprint-like" hackathon of just five days and to create a simple step-by-step guide to its implementation. According to the authors, this condensation and focus protects the entrepreneurs from getting lost in the daily chaos of "endless email, deadlines that slip, meetings that burn up your day, and long-term projects based on questionable assumptions" (Knapp *et al.* 2016, p. 9).

In this so-called "sprint week", entrepreneurs aspiring to get funded by GV would go through the following steps:

– **Monday**: understanding the problem/need by carefully developing a Customer Journey Map and planning the testing stage on Friday.

– **Tuesday**: examining competing solutions by sketching and storyboarding ideas.

– **Wednesday**: deciding on the best solution by using a silent voting system and planning the prototyping stage on Thursday.

– **Thursday**: building a realistic prototype.

– **Friday**: testing prototype using in-depth interviews with five target customers.

We have used a simplified version of Knapp's Design Sprint in a classroom environment to demonstrate Design Thinking and Lean Startup principles using the steps below.

5.5.1. *Creating an authentic sprint environment*

"Think of a digital product or service from a company you admire and imagine ways to improve it by identifying pain points in the current customer journey, then prototyping a better app interface to address these pains and finally by testing your solution." This is the challenge I give my innovation students every year to make them apply the principles of Design Thinking and Lean Startup.

They often choose companies like Apple, Google, Netflix and Amazon, due to their digital presence and high innovation reputation. Ideally, groups should be kept small for this activity, with clearly defined roles: UX expert (understanding the User eXperience and developing a Customer Journey Map), UI expert (designing the User Interface using special prototyping tools) and a VL specialist (a Validated Learning expert to design the testing phase). See the next section for more details on the deliverables of each role.

Creating this challenge environment before presenting the frameworks has the benefit of getting students to reflect on their roles and their projects as each new tool is presented. This, in my experience, leads them to become more engaged and ask questions about the tools as they are unfolded and to make sure they understand how they work in the context of their project.

5.5.2. *Reflecting about the simplified design sprint framework*

All the figures of this chapter could become slides for an effective course on the evolution of the product development process. The conceptual class could start by explaining the stage-gate process and its shortcomings, and then discuss the Customer Development process and how it was a precursor to the Design Thinking and Lean Startup principles. After these two principles are explained, a concrete project can be proposed based on a Simplified Design Sprint Framework (illustrated in Figure 5.8). If only a few hours are available to cover this subject, students should develop a project that applies the three key steps derived from Knapp's original method, namely:

– empathizing with the pain points of the client or user using a Customer Journey Map;

– developing a very simple prototype that addresses those unmet needs;

– testing it with a select group of target consumers.

A Customer Journey Map (CJM) is a graphical depiction of the touchpoints between the user and the brand. It defines the overall customer experience for the positive moments (gains) and negative ones (pains). Identifying pain points (moments of frustration, friction, unpleasant moments) in the customer experience is essential to improve it. This must be done from the functional, emotional and social perspectives. Figure 5.9, created by a group of my students led by Manon Ray in 2019, illustrates an example of CJM highlighting the touchpoints in the context of a PayPal project to reward users based on their ability to develop an active lifestyle. The objective of the project was to increase the awareness of PayPal services and to associate the services with a healthier lifestyle. In order to understand which critical touchpoints would be impacted by the project, Manon and her colleagues researched how a PayPal customer interacts with the brand at various levels through their actions (doing), emotions (feelings) and functional expectations (thinking). Then, they identified opportunities to imagine how their "step-by-step saving" program could be integrated into the PayPal service.

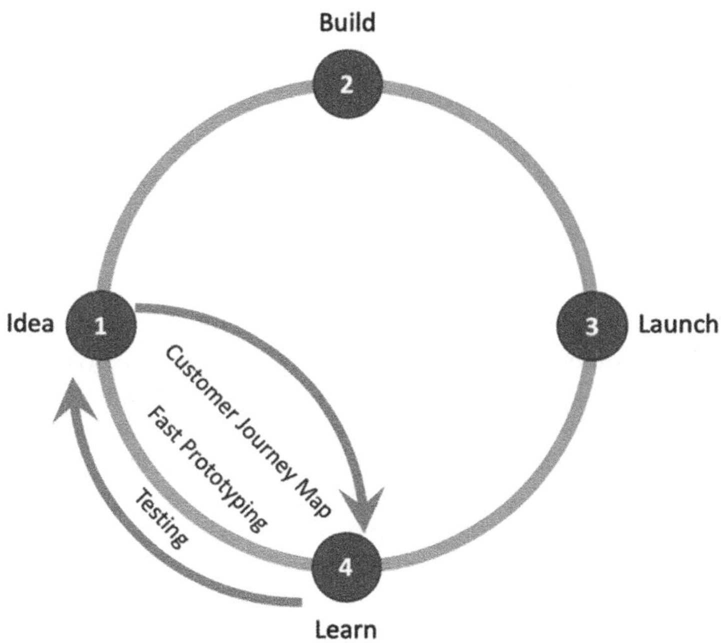

Figure 5.8. *Simplified design sprint stages (adapted from Knapp* et al. *2016). For a color version of the figure, see http://www.iste.co.uk/lima/entrepreneurship.zip*

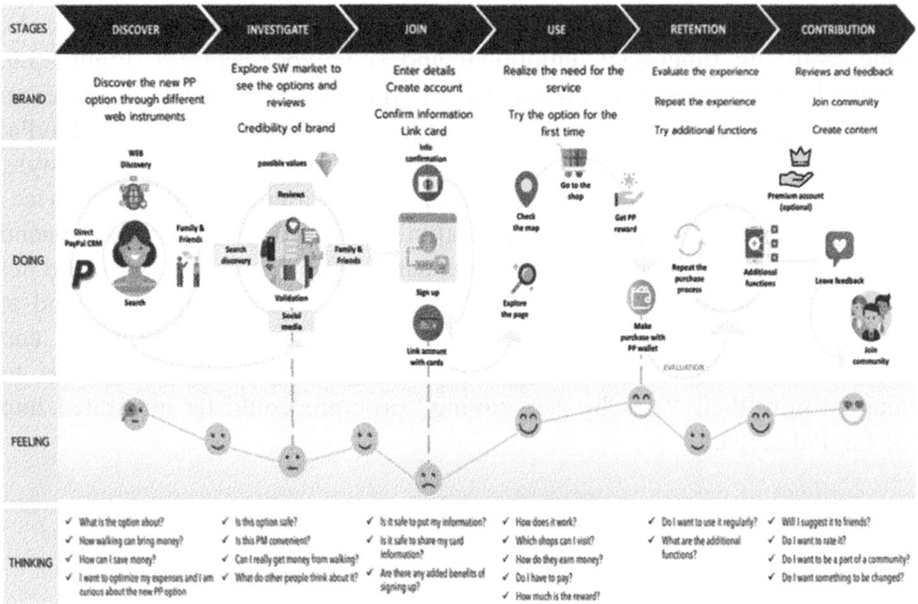

Figure 5.9. *Example of CJM created by student Manon Ray and a group of colleagues in an innovation class at Skema Business School (reproduced with permission from the authors). For a color version of the figure, see http://www.iste.co.uk/lima/entrepreneurship.zip*

Thanks to this kind of map, we can see in Manon's example that one of the main pain points of the system is in the discovery, investigation and signing up stages. These could become the focus of the innovation effort. The students can now discuss how their service innovation can be used to attract new users and earn their loyalty by encouraging them to link up their account to their favorite activity tracking app/accessory (most smartphones have the ability to measure daily steps). They can also discuss how to make this process as frictionless and pleasant as possible.

5.5.3. *Using technology to make it more interactive and collaborative*

Free (or freemium) online tools can help students enjoy a hands-on approach to this kind of project. The three tools we have been using in our Design Thinking classes are Smaply, Marvel and Lookback.

– **Smaply.com** can help students create a balanced CJM and facilitate collaboration to develop it. It displays a very intuitive interface that allows students to create strips based on the emotional, functional and cognitive journeys of their targeted consumers and to insert icons, pictures and text to illustrate them.

– **Marvelapp.com** facilitates the design of very credible digital app prototypes with no previous design experience. We can start from scratch and use rudimentary wireframe solutions to design early stage prototypes. Students can also start from screen shots of existing apps and use solutions like Photoshop, GIMP or even PowerPoint to alter the layout of these pages, adding new buttons and icons to give the illusion of functionality. Once these background images are ready, all they have to do is upload them to Marvel and create "hotspots" around clickable areas, linking them to designated pages (such as interactive menus, merchandise display and checkout area). This is not very much different than creating interactive PowerPoint slides, and students usually learn how to do this in less than one hour of playing with the platform.

– **Lookback.io** is an intuitive platform for testing smartphone app prototypes. It allows students to collect qualitative data and live feedback about their prototypes either on face-to-face situations or from remote users. It uses the selfie camera of smartphones to film the facial expressions of testers, while recording the screen and every interaction with the user. If students do not have time to actually do the testing of their app with Lookback, they can at least present their test design and a sample test with one person in the group using this app.

One can find several tutorials on how to use these tools (or their competitors) on the Web. Figuring out how to use them is part of the fun for students. My advice is to present the tools very briefly using a web video and then to let students try to apply them to their projects in small groups. Having separate roles for the different tools in each group may give more accountability to this experience (while making it more fun!).

6

Scaling Up: The Challenges of Knowledge Management

This chapter discusses how a knowledge management framework can help startups continue to innovate as they grow, using examples and best practices from companies that have successfully scaled up[1]. The knowledge management framework we use here is derived from McKinsey's classic 7S approach to examine how elements of strategy, structure and systems contribute to creating a culture of innovation. Before we do so, we define the basic elements in a management system. We highlight how people and information are the two most valuable resources for innovation management, as these are two necessary components for knowledge creation. We then proceed to discuss how innovative organizations should focus on the strategic and tactical elements of knowledge management, while using information systems as a support for communication and control. We finally apply all of these elements in specific discussions of critical incidents involving several leading organizations in the last decades.

If a business student were asked to describe a complex organization, such as Apple Inc., he or she might be tempted to talk about well-known, trivial aspects of that iconic company, such as its location in California, its product line, its brand reputation and its charismatic founder and historic CEO Steve Jobs. Usually, though, students quickly run out of elements to describe Apple or any other organization, even ones they are very much familiar with, like their own business school or the firm where they are doing their

1 This chapter was adapted from a passage originally published by the author in Lima and Nivet (2015).

internship. The reason for such lack of depth is that the human mind tends to focus on only a few aspects of any problem at any given time. Hence, frameworks play such an important role in business learning. As we have seen throughout this book, a framework can be simply defined as a "checklist" for thinking (Lima and Fabiani 2014).

Consider, for example, organizational analysis frameworks. If we break down the above question with the help of a classic framework, such as McKinsey's 7S model (structure, strategy, systems, staff, skills, style and shared values), a student will be able to ask more specific questions, such as "What is Apple's *strategy* in the smartphone market?" or "How does Apple use its *structure* to incentivize creativity among its engineers?" or "What are some of Apple's *staff* recruiting criteria?" These framework-based questions are a meaningful guide to understanding the complexity of organizations as they grow.

6.1. An overview of management systems

Before discussing how innovative organizations can use the 7S framework for knowledge management, it is convenient to recall the basic definitions of *management* in general and *innovation management* in particular. A question that even advanced students sometimes struggle to thoroughly answer is, how can we define any type of management process – project management, knowledge management, innovation management etc.? While some of their answers capture some of the aspects of management, students rarely have a systemic view of the management process. Based on the classic PDCA cycle or "Deming Wheel", Figure 6.1 illustrates the key elements of a simple management system.

The PDCA principles are nothing new. In fact, they can be traced back all the way to the creation of the Scientific Method by Francis Bacon in the 17th Century, whose "hypothesize–experiment–evaluate" process is very similar. What makes management a particular "science" is that it consists of planning, allocating and controlling a very particular set of *resources* (Platje and Wadman 1998; Singh 2013). These resources mainly consist of four essential components: human, informational, financial and material elements (Davenport 2013). Arguably, human and informational resources are the most important of these components. Indeed, if we have the right people, they will use the most relevant strategic sources of information to generate knowledge and intelligent decisions about financial and material resources required to deliver value to customers. Conversely, having a lot of money or materials but poor decision-makers will not get organizations very far.

Consider, for example, the case of Facebook. Mark Zuckerberg did not have a lot of money, infrastructure or personnel when he started his company in a Harvard dormitory. However, because he had the right vision and knowledge, and because he knew the right *people* (other developers, venture capitalists, experienced entrepreneurs), he could get all the other resources required to build the most successful social network in the history of the Internet.

Figure 6.1 summarizes what might be called the "DNA of every managerial problem". As discussed above, management problems occur either because of poor planning, or due to implementation or controlling of people, information, money or materials. As simple as it is, this insight is a powerful way of identifying internal strengths and weaknesses in a managerial system, whether they deal with innovation management, HR management, IT management, logistics or finance. Like the DNA molecules that constitute all living things – microscopic or gigantic – these elements are the basis of every organizational process, whether we are talking about a one-person startup or a multi-billion-dollar business conglomerate.

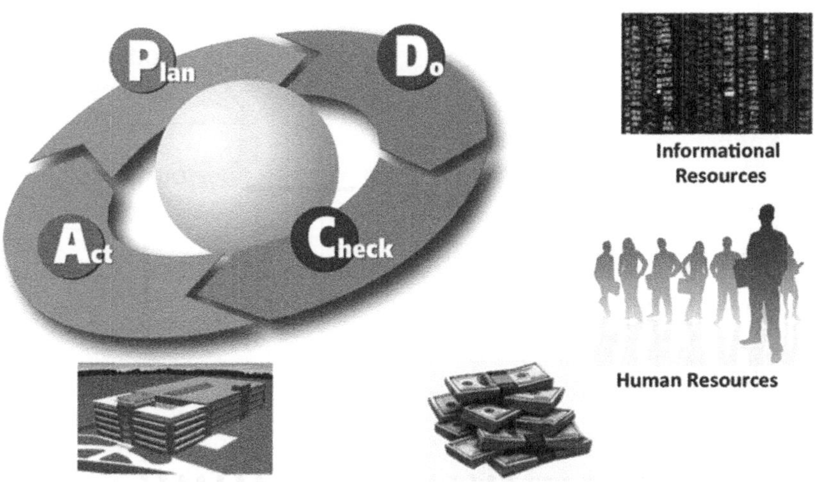

Figure 6.1. *The "DNA" of management problems. For a color version of the figure, see http://www.iste.co.uk/lima/entrepreneurship.zip*

Therefore, we can revisit our definition of innovation management as the process of planning, implementing and controlling knowledge (people + information) in order to create product and services that address certain *unmet needs of the market*. This definition introduces an external component, market needs and expectations, which is beyond the direct control of managers. Hence, good innovation managers are competent not only in dealing with the internal resources at their disposal, but also at understanding those poorly met market needs and expectations and to devise solutions for them (see Chapter 3 for a detailed discussion of internal and external variables in a management system).

Every basic system is composed of four basic elements: input, process, output and feedback (Ilgen *et al.* 2005). In a management system, as illustrated in Figure 6.2, inputs typically consist of the aforementioned resources (human, informational, financial and material). The process is defined by the stages of planning, allocating and controlling those resources in order to create outputs (products or services) that address customer needs. This approach is often called the "Resource-based View of the Firm" (Barney *et al.* 2001). Market feedback is the signal (in the form of product adoption rates, comments, criticisms) generated by customers who buy and/or use the product, as well as information concerning opportunities of doing a better job than competitors at solving current and future customer needs.

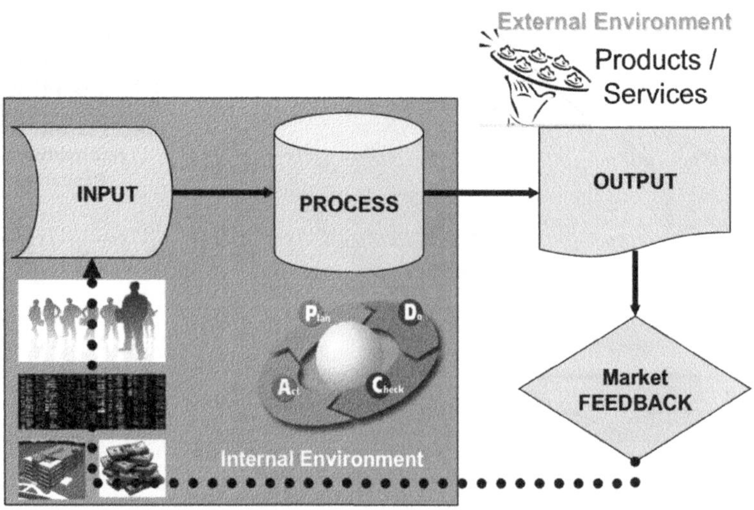

Figure 6.2. *Illustration of a management system. For a color version of the figure, see http://www.iste.co.uk/lima/entrepreneurship.zip*

Great companies are very good at listening to market feedback and adapting their inputs and processes to bridge the gap between customer needs and the firm's actual output. They behave like an open system, in which the conditions of the external environment directly influence how inputs and processes are managed – like an air conditioner that adjusts how much cold air it produces based on the readings of the thermostat and the desired temperature established by the user. Mediocre companies find it difficult to learn with the external environment and adapt its resources and processes accordingly, behaving like a closed system – like a ventilator that keeps the air flow steady at one level irrespective of the changes in external temperatures.

The examples of Nokia and Blackberry are very eloquent when it comes to illustrating the dangers of not listening to market needs/feedback and adapting its processes accordingly. By sticking to the idea that physical keyboards were a necessary element of smartphones, even after market feedback showed how the world craved tactile devices, these two companies basically signed their death sentences. Samsung, on the contrary, realized that this new market trend was irreversible very early on, and partnered with Google to develop tactile Android phones to compete directly with Apple.

6.2. The 7S framework for organizational analysis

Now that the basic elements of every managerial system are established, let us revisit the internal (thus controllable) elements of business environments. In Chapter 3, we used Porter's Value Chain framework to look at primary activities (inbound logistics, process, outbound logistics, marketing, after sales) and secondary activities (technology, finance, human resources, infrastructure). These can be understood as systems for managing the four resources mentioned above. Porter's framework is useful to distinguish between the primary and supporting systems, but it fails to portray other elements that affect organizational performance: strategy, structure and culture. As we also saw in Chapter 3, before the Resource-based View of the Firm was popularized by Barnes *et al.* (2001), the consulting firm McKinsey & Company created a framework that was very well adapted to that purpose, known as the "7S" framework (Waterman *et al.* 1980), shown in Figure 6.3.

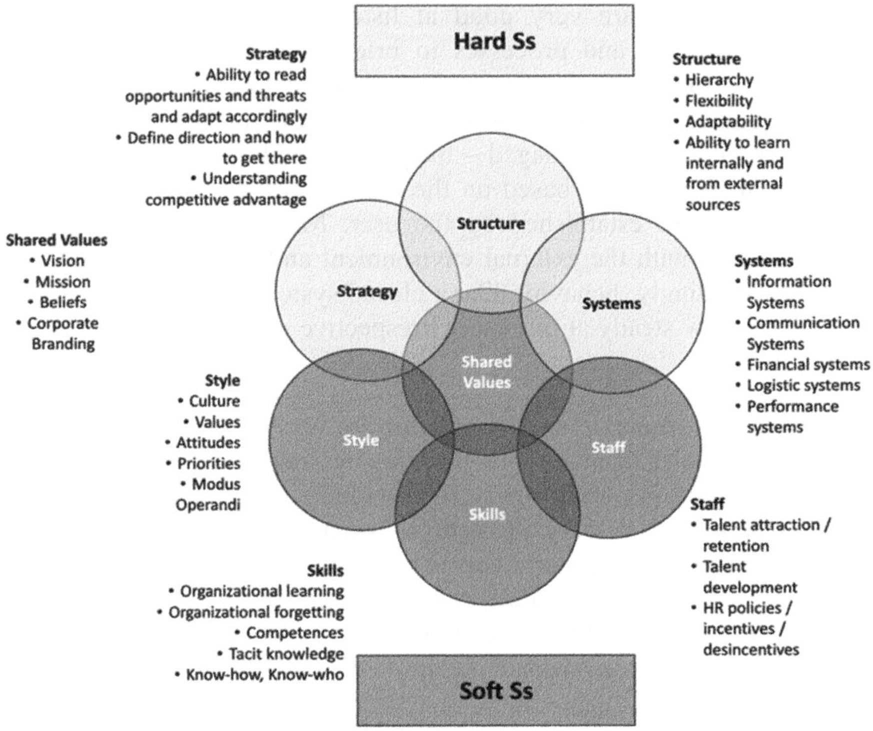

Figure 6.3. *Revisiting McKinsey's 7S framework. For a color version of the figure, see http://www.iste.co.uk/lima/entrepreneurship.zip*

The first thing to note in this approach is the fact that these variables are all interdependent and non-hierarchical (as suggested by the interconnected lines). A change in *strategy* will affect the way communication and control *systems* are used, for example, as well as the way people use the formal and informal *structures* to develop projects, the skills that will be prioritized, the people/*staff* who will play the most important role and, ultimately, how the organizational culture (*shared values/style*) will be affected. Conversely, recruiting new people (staff) or introducing new tools or systems will provoke changes in the organization's DNA that will eventually cause all the other variables to adapt, and so on.

Another important aspect of this framework is the fact that certain variables are more easily controllable than others. Strategy, structure and systems are called "hard Ss" because, just like the "hard sciences" (physics, chemistry, mathematics), they can be quantifiable or at least explained by using explicit supports (diagrams, charts, slides, etc.). The "soft Ss", however, belong to the sphere of the intangible, implicit domain of organizational culture (staff/people, management style, skills, shared values). It is much easier to design the strategy, the structure and the systems of an organization than to "develop" its "soft" aspects. When it comes to innovation, however, a close coordination between soft and hard elements is crucial for creating or developing a learning environment, as explained below.

6.3. Towards a framework for innovative knowledge management

In the early 2000s, an ex-McKinsey consultant called Claudio Terra created a model for innovation and knowledge management based on the classic 7S framework, which is shown in Figure 6.4.

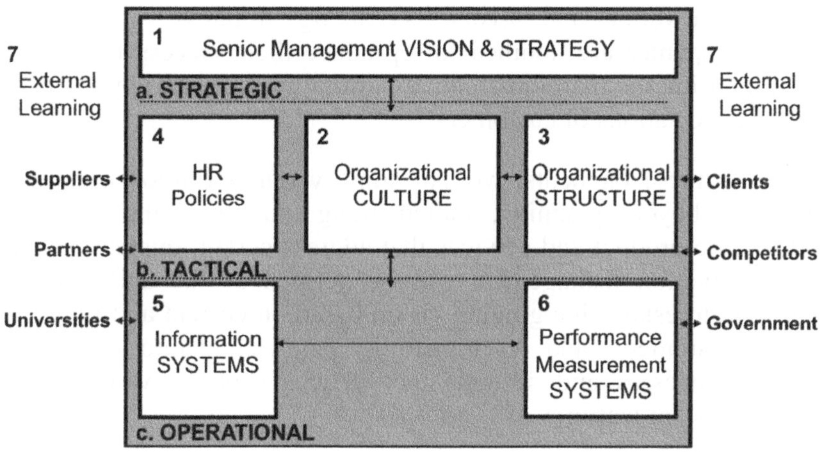

Figure 6.4. *The seven dimensions of knowledge management (Terra, 2001). For a color version of the figure, see http://www.iste.co.uk/lima/entrepreneurship.zip*

Terra's diagram has the merit of prioritizing the strategic, tactical and operational variables of the McKinsey model while adding a distinction between internal and external learning environments. The similarities and distinctions between the two models become clear at a glance: strategy (and vision, element number 1) becomes the most important layer. It is an "umbrella" overhanging all other variables; the rise or fall of organizations largely depends on how accurate and flexible their senior management vision and strategy are.

Culture (2) is the equivalent to style and shared values. Structure (3) remains a separate component, while staff and skills become HR Policies (4). Systems are subdivided into information systems (5) and performance measurement systems (6), emphasizing the importance of communication and control in learning organizations. Moreover, external learning (7) is added. We also see here how two of the input elements previously discussed in a management system are particularly prominent: people (4) and information (5), the basis of learning and knowledge creation (7). Furthermore, two of the management process variables are emphasized: planning (vision, strategy, number 1) and control (performance measurement, number 6).

It is worth mentioning the central role of culture (2) in Terra's model: after vision and strategy, it is the second most important piece of his whole concept. All other elements in the organization converge to create and influence organizational culture, but as suggested by the double headed arrows, they are all equally influenced by those "shared values". Without a culture of innovation that favors risk taking, initiative and iconoclastic thinking, companies are doomed to reproduce their success formulas from the past, ignoring the many learning opportunities presented by the evolving needs and expectations of customers.

Based on these elements, we can amplify our definition of innovation management: beyond planning, implementing and controlling knowledge in order to create product and services that address certain unmet needs of the market, innovation management can be defined as the ability of senior management to establish a guiding vision based on current and future unmet needs of customers, and to transform that vision into organizational structures, processes and systems that deliver superior value through a culture of constant learning.

In the following section, we will illustrate this definition by revisiting each one of the elements in Terra's framework in the context of best practices by leading companies.

6.4. Applying Terra's framework: best practices from leading companies

6.4.1. *Senior management vision and strategy*

When he co-created the first commercially successful personal computer in 1976, the Apple II, Steve Jobs had a vision of "computers for ordinary people" that seemed completely absurd at the time. Hewlett-Packard, which technically had the intellectual property rights to the prototype created from its spare parts, dismissed it as a child's toy with no practical use. Apple had raised 250,000 dollars in venture capital, allowing it to go from a garage business to a promising startup. But rather than put all the money into finished products, most of the initial budget was used for prototyping a machine that looked and felt as friendly as a household appliance and to communicate about its features in a very high-end advertising campaign. This strategy paid off handsomely when the product was launched at the West Coast Computer Fair of 1977. The vision of computers made accessible to ordinary people through meticulously user-friendly design, coupled with a strategy to position itself as a premium, high-margin brand, made Apple one of the most iconic companies of all time.

During the same period, Microsoft also had a vision of "a computer on every desktop and Microsoft software running every computer". Their strategy, however, would involve less focus on the user experience and more focus on the business model. Rather than obsess with product perfection, like Steve Jobs, Bill Gates focused on creating strategic partnerships (with IBM initially, then with Original Equipment Manufacturers) to make sure that every new computer would leave the factory with Microsoft software in it. By retaining ownership of the software (in other words by licensing rather than selling it), Microsoft created an innovative business model with high revenue streams and low costs, thus becoming one of the most prosperous players in the personal computer revolution.

A great vision without a coherent innovation strategy, or vice versa, will most likely lead to failure. Kodak went bankrupt not for lack of innovation culture or because they failed to launch new products and services (they actually invented the first digital camera), but because they underestimated the rate of obsolescence of their core product, chemical films. Conversely, visionary startups fail every day because they lack an appropriate go-to-market strategy or business plan.

6.4.2. *Culture, structure and human resource policies*

These three components are intimately related and can be said to be directly connected with vision and strategy. Let us take Apple's example again. In order to fulfill his vision of creating beautifully designed products that anybody can use, Steve Jobs knew he needed "artists". In his own words[2], "part of what made the Macintosh great was that the people working on it were musicians and poets and artists and zoologists and historians who also happened to be the best computer scientists in the world". Apple's recruitment policies were deeply influenced by a culture "at the crossroads of engineering and liberal arts". It is not only the kinds of talents they recruited and how they retained them, but also how their offices were designed to allow a free flow of communication across open spaces, the way people were encouraged to work in small teams and the way new ideas were appreciated and stimulated. Apple's current "spaceship" headquarters in Cupertino, California, is a good example of how these cultural values permeate its organizational structure.

From the design of these headquarters, we can immediately apprehend that

– the circular shape of the building suggests a flat-hierarchy ethos;

– the presence of green spaces and ubiquitous sun-filled rooms indicates how much the company values employee well-being as a source of creative thinking;

– the "walkable" nature of the circumference and the prominent role of the cafeteria suggests that well-designed physical layouts facilitate serendipity, chance meetings, casual sharing, collision of ideas and "cross-fertilization" of creative minds.

All of these structural elements aim to avoid the "silos" syndrome of large corporations – different parts of a company that hardly ever meet spontaneously to coordinate and exchange ideas. Of course, a physical building is not the cause but the symptom of a culture of learning and innovation. Active human resources policies (such as recruitment and career development criteria, training, motivation techniques, etc.) should stimulate cross-functional exchange and incentivize team work in order to fully develop a culture of creative collaboration.

6.4.3. *Information systems and performance measurement systems*

Information technology (IT) as a tool to reduce costs and improve performance is at the heart of most innovations created by Amazon. At the world's largest online retailer, IT algorithms are used, for instance, as follows:

2 http://www.pbs.org/nerds/part3.html.

– to facilitate customer decision-making through search and recommendation engines at https://www.amazon.com/;

– to improve logistics by tracking packages and determining optimum inventory levels according to demand;

– to reduce travel costs by promoting videoconferencing and distant collaboration;

– to create a dashboard of instant metrics, from the average time spent on the phone during customer service calls to sales forecasts.

Like Google, which is reputed for basing every product decision on data, Amazon has achieved their world dominance through a careful combination of technology and controlling systems. Jeff Bezos, Amazon's CEO, created a culture of "decision by metrics" that permeates every meeting throughout the company. Those metrics take into account not just the financial aspects of the business, but also customer, process and learning performance indicators, as popularized by Kaplan and Norton's (1996) Balanced Scorecard (BSC, shown in Figure 6.5).

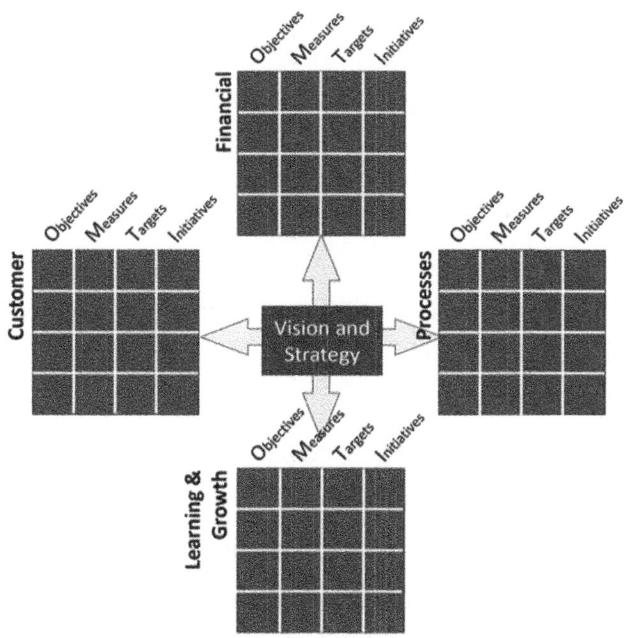

Figure 6.5. *The Balanced Scorecard (adapted from Kaplan and Norton 1996). For a color version of the figure, see http://www.iste.co.uk/lima/entrepreneurship.zip*

The BSC was created with the notion that multiple dimensions are involved in business development. Making business decisions based only on financial data (past sales, growth trends, etc.) is like driving a car through the rear-view mirror. The BSC helps managers and entrepreneurs think in a multidimensional framework structured around the following sets of questions:

– How should we appear to our shareholders/investors? Examples of key financial metrics include:

- return on investment;
- cash flow;
- return on capital employed;
- financial results (quarterly/yearly);
- internal business processes.

– What activities should we excel at? Examples of key business process metrics include:

- rate of on-time delivery;
- order fulfillment time;
- rates of capacity utilization;
- yield measurements;
- percentage of project cost variance;
- employee productivity.

– How will we sustain our ability to change and improve? Some key learning and growth metrics are:

- employee turnover;
- job satisfaction;
- training/learning opportunities;
- percentage of revenue from new products/services;
- engagement rate in innovation projects.

– How should we appear to our targeted segments? Key customer metrics could include, for example:

- perceived brand attributes;
- customer satisfaction rate;
- customer percentage of market;
- customer retention rate.

Each company should create their own set of relevant indicators based on their industry best practices. The answers to each one of these questions should be inspired by the original vision and strategy of the firm, to make sure the used metrics are relevant and contributing to a move in the right direction. This reinforces the importance of the strategic element in Terra's original model as the "starting point" and "overarching principle" that should guide every organizational dimension. It also reinforces the link between planning, allocation and controlling of resources as the basis of every management system.

It should be noted, however, that not everything can be measured and controlled. Personal judgment and "gut instincts" do play an important role in moving towards the vision. Einstein did not have any empirical data when he first formulated his theory of relativity – he famously stated that imagination is more important than knowledge. Therefore, it is appropriate that information and control systems remain at the operational level of Terra's framework, entirely subordinate to the strategic and tactical levels. Even though the "hard Ss" (strategy, structure, systems) can and should be measured, the intangible "soft Ss" (skills, staff, shared values and style), which are part of the human side of organizations, are difficult to measure and yet remain essential for the innovation process to succeed.

6.4.4. *Learning with the external environment*

The final dimension in Terra's framework, learning with suppliers, partners, customers and competitors, adds the external environment to the original 7S framework. Indeed, innovation cannot happen if internal learning is disconnected from outside sources. Unmet customer needs are, as seen, the very essence of what drives innovations, but meeting those needs requires both a "knowledge push" (introducing product and service features based on a firm's own technology and competences) and "market pull" (learning from customers, competitors, research centers, government agencies, suppliers and partners).

The story of the introduction of graphic user interfaces (GUIs) in the personal computing revolution is quite emblematic of how these learning opportunities interplay. Xerox was the first company to adapt a mouse as an input device for a graphic screen when it created the Xerox Alto computer prototype in the late 1970s. In another example of the importance of vision for innovation success, Xerox leaders did not see how the new machine related to their core business of document management. They therefore agreed to let Steve Jobs use the technology in the first Macintosh computer in 1984. The Macintosh interface in turn inspired Microsoft to create Windows, which remains the most widely used operating system to this date.

The saga of GUIs illustrates how vision, strategy and external learning are closely related. Such a technological breakthrough could not have come from a "market pull" initiative, such as developing a customer survey. It required visionary leaders such as Jobs and Gates to adopt it as a "knowledge push" movement. Xerox, Apple and Microsoft illustrate how partners can become competitors and competitors can become suppliers in the learning game. Because Microsoft had a better business model than Apple and because it was better positioned than Xerox, it reaped far more benefits from the GUI revolution than its inventors and pioneers. Constantly monitoring what was happening in Silicon Valley was a key factor that explains Microsoft success as an innovator.

6.5. Knowledge management in the ecosystem: Quintuple Helix and stakeholder maps

In order to scale up, businesses must learn from the external ecosystem in order to constantly adapt their strategies, structure and systems. Even their culture (style and shared values) must evolve if a company is to adapt their skills and staff profile to ever-changing competitive environments. Terra's seventh dimension (learning with the external environment) offers a checklist of the key players that businesses must monitor to ensure they are constantly learning from customers, competitors, suppliers, partners, research centers and universities.

As mentioned in Chapter 1, Carayannis *et al.* (2012) offer an even more comprehensive framework for analyzing the collaboration opportunities in the innovation ecosystem. Figure 6.6 reproduces the adaptation of the concept of Quintuple Helix. In it, we see how sustainable development/growth can be achieved through innovation; in order to be innovative, companies need to learn from their own competitive environment (the economic system where the "entrepreneurial capital" stems from). They must also constantly interact and learn from universities and research centers (sources of human capital). The government can be a key player in this environment, offering financial support, data and networks. Thus, companies must not only keep informed of government policies concerning innovation and economic development, but also actively participate in government-sponsored activities in bodies such as embassies, chambers of commerce and public agencies.

In a digitally connected world, in which any private citizen can make or break a brand with a tweet or a Facebook post, it has become more necessary than ever to monitor the attitudes of the general public as a key stakeholder. An important subset of this group is, of course, the company's direct customers. The way a company and its products are perceived are important not just in terms of reputation (social capital) but also as a source of learning about unmet needs and expectations.

The final dimension of Carayannis' model is the natural environment. Ecological constraints are an increasingly important component in any company's strategy. Learning how to reduce one's impact on the environment (thus increasing one's "natural capital") could be a powerful source of innovation.

This multitude of stakeholders could easily lead a company to lose focus and to spread its scarce informational resources over too large a field of intelligence gathering. As usual, some sort of prioritization framework is necessary to help decision-makers focus on the key players in the external environment. Stakeholder mapping, shown in Figure 6.7, is a commonly used tool to prioritize sources of learning from the ecosystem. First introduced by Mendelow (1981), this four-by-four matrix creates four profiles of stakeholders in an ecosystem:

– **Static powerless**: These are actors who are unlikely to be an interesting source of opportunities or threats. They should be mostly ignored.

– **Dynamic powerless**: Even though these actors cannot affect the business directly due to their low power, they are highly dynamic and could be an important source of learning, benchmarking. Potential partnerships could emerge here.

– **Static powerful**: These are well-established players who change little over time. Though highly strategic, their static nature justifies saving resources by monitoring them only periodically.

– **Dynamic powerful**: These are the key players in your field. These are "movers and shakers". It is essential to create partnerships with them and to constantly learn from their best practices.

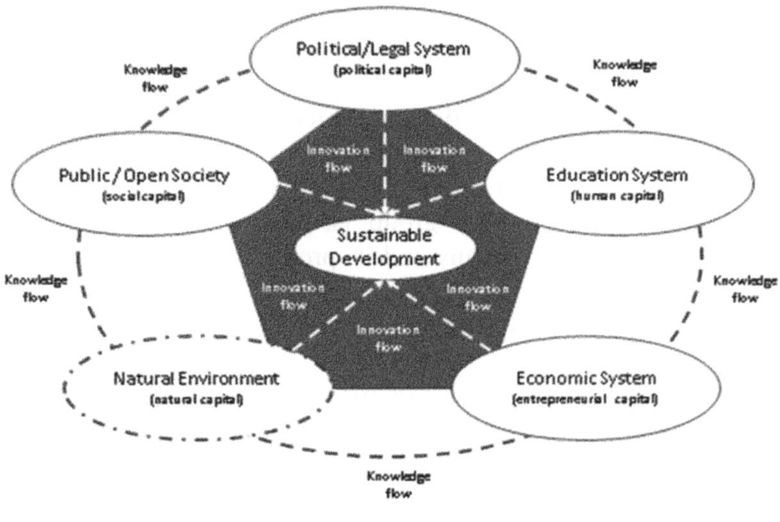

Figure 6.6. *Revisiting the Quintuple Helix of knowledge flow in innovation ecosystems (adapted from Carayannis* et al. *2012).*

6.6. Teaching and learning knowledge management

In this chapter, we tried to synthesize through a few key images and examples how the use of frameworks can make it easier to understand the role of strategy (and vision), structure and systems in innovation management. We tried to demonstrate that an innovation management system consists, like any other management process, of planning, allocating and controlling resources. The ability of an organization to learn and use knowledge (people + information) to address the unmet needs of customers is what distinguishes innovation from other processes.

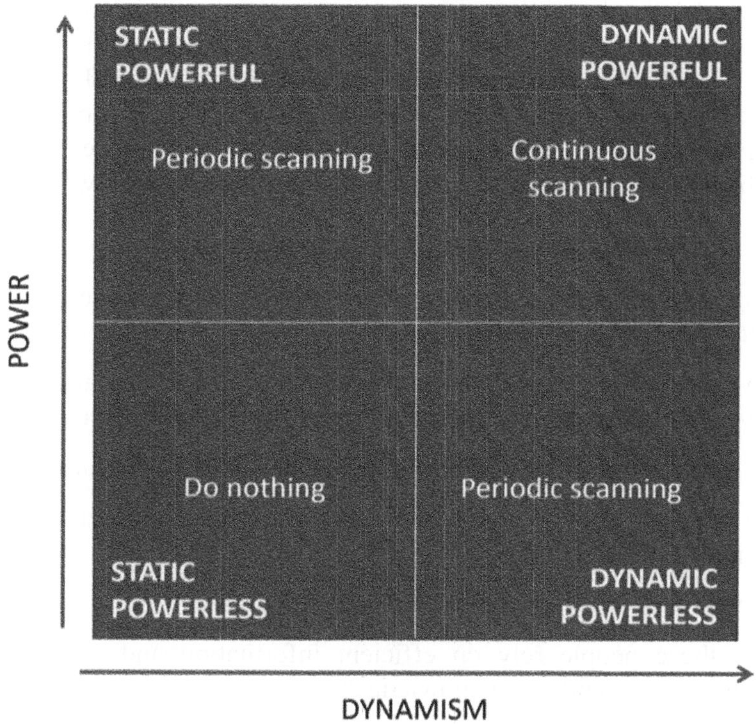

Figure 6.7. *Stakeholder priority mapping (adapted from Mendelow 1981). For a color version of the figure, see http://www.iste.co.uk/lima/entrepreneurship.zip*

Terra's framework, based on McKinsey's original 7S model, integrates these variables beautifully. It gives a prominent role to strategy and vision as the starting point of every innovation process. Vision and strategy are, as seen, supported by structures and systems in tactical and operational levels. Innovative organizations are designed to appropriately adapt each one of these components in order to maximize learning from the external environment. The Quintuple Helix and the stakeholder mapping tools can help identify all the stakeholders in the ecosystem and prioritize them.

For the sake of synthesis, some of the interesting relationships between the variables are simplified or omitted here. The best way to internalize the frameworks presented in this chapter is to practice them. After introducing Terra's model, teachers may encourage students to work in small groups to interview startup founders and to diagnose their "knowledge management maturity" level using the conceptual lenses discussed here. The "checklists for thinking" in this chapter should make it easier to identify problems in the learning processes of those organizations and how to propose solutions on how to better manage resources to promote innovation and growth.

Here are a few questions that may help in this process:

– Do they have a clear vision of their role in fulfilling unmet needs and a coherent strategy to deliver that value?

– Do they have a culture that prioritizes constant learning and adaptation to the ever changing opportunities and threats of the external environment?

– Do their organizational structures facilitate sharing and learning?

– Do they recruit the right people, with the right competences to fulfill their vision?

– Are these people incentivized to learn and grow?

– Can these people rely on efficient information and communication systems to produce and share knowledge?

– Are the performance metrics relevant and attuned to the vision and strategy?

– Is this organization capable of constantly adapting its processes and outputs based on feedback from the actors in the external environment (above all customers, and also partners, suppliers and competitors)?

After interviewing one CEO or startup founder using this interview guide, each group should meet and debrief their findings. If they had permission to film the interviews, they could use online tools such as Microsoft Stream or YouTube Studio to automatically obtain a transcript of the interviews (as downloadable closed captions from the uploaded videos). A synthesis of these transcripts can then be parsed on a collaborative spreadsheet, as shown in Table 6.1.

Category	Group 1	Group 2	Group n	Horizontal synthesis
Vision and strategy				
Culture				
HR				
Structure				
Information and communication systems				
Performance measurement systems				
Learning with the external environment				
Vertical synthesis				

Table 6.1. *Vertical and horizontal table for qualitative data analysis and synthesis*

A vertical analysis of each column would give a synthesis of the strengths and weaknesses of each startup on the last line of the table ("Vertical synthesis"). A horizontal analysis would allow students to compare differences between the several testimonials, giving an overview of typical difficulties faced by these startups in their knowledge management process. If done well, the horizontal analysis could become an eloquent portrayal of typical pitfalls and barriers that hinder startup innovation and growth.

7

Epilogue: Insights from Twenty Years of Teaching E&I

Our first article about E&I was published 20 years ago (Lima and Dolabela 2000). Since then, I have written a PhD dissertation about the potential of technology to support business education (Lima 2003; Lima *et al.* 2004) and several articles dealing directly or indirectly with this core subject of my research. Examples of related themes in my publications include: innovation ecosystems (Lima 2001; Laperche *et al.* 2019) and technology parks (Lima and Hastenreiter 2008; Lima *et al.* 2008), the use of case studies in business education (Lima and Fabiani 2014, 2016), entrepreneurial traits (Namaci *et al.* 2013), the use of Osterwalder's Business Model Canvas in education (Lima and Baudier 2017; Lima *et al.* 2018), entrepreneurship teaching (Albertini *et al.* 2019) and innovation in smart cities or smart organizations (Appio *et al.* 2019; Lima 2020).

After 20 years of teaching and researching this topic, as this book hopes to have shown, a few core ideas have emerged that could contribute to the debate on how to adapt the teaching and learning of entrepreneurship and innovation to the challenges and opportunities of the 21st Century. This final chapter summarizes these insights by discussing how the principles of Collaborative Interactivity have underpinned each one of the teaching strategies suggested throughout this book.

7.1. Learning by reflecting about authentic situations

This long experience with case studies has taught us that, in ill-structured knowledge domains such as entrepreneurship and innovation management, abstract frameworks are meaningless without concrete examples. One does not necessarily have to use the 20-page long classical Harvard-style case studies, but a multitude of short cases, preferably created by students from their own research as they play the roles of CEOs, CMOs and CTOs of successful companies whose best practices they are trying to emulate. Doing what the French call "*mise en situation*" (literally "put in the situation") is a powerful way to get students to think critically about concrete problems while coming up with their own solutions. In this process, they need some sort of "intellectual structure" to help them cover all the aspects of the situation, a checklist for making sense of multidimensional problems.

Thus, combining multiple frameworks with bottom-up case studies is a very effective way of helping students develop their critical and creative thinking skills, while at the same time giving them the means to synthesize their solutions to each other or before an audience. Taking turns exposing their "cases" to the rest of the class and hearing feedback from both the teacher and the other students exposes the learners to a large variety of situations and perspectives, while consolidating their ability to use heuristic tools to make sense of very complex knowledge domains.

7.2. Learning by collaboration

Out of the four pillars of the Collaborative Interactivity principles exemplified in this book, collaboration is probably the most important in E&I education. Indeed, creating a new venture or innovating in an existing business is not a solitary endeavor. It requires sharing one's ideas, enriching them with other people's vision, recognizing one's own biases and taking into account different perspectives in the process of new product development. In our E&I classes, we have systematically asked students to create groups of no more than five and no less than four members. Like mentioned previously, it is sometimes quite effective to suggest that they choose roles in the decision-making process (a design specialist, a marketing expert, a supply chain manager, etc.). Of course, in a startup, these roles are often played by the same person; however, separating them for the sake of the group work gives students a certain sense of ownership and empowers them to become experts in one part of the problem.

We have always been fascinated by the tale of a group of blind men touching an elephant for the first time and trying to guess what the animal looks like. One of them touches the trunk and believes that an elephant looks like a serpent, the other touches the tail and thinks that it is more like a rope. A third one touches a leg and says that the beast looks like a tree trunk, while a fourth touches the belly and affirms that the others are all wrong, the elephant is more like a whale. The truth is that they are all individually wrong and collectively right: put together all the elements described, and they will get a fairly accurate idea of the shape of the elephant.

Students, like all of us, are loaded with biases and prejudices related to their own life's story, their gender privileges or struggles, their social class and their own personality. Putting them in a situation in which they have to be confronted with these biases in order to negotiate a shared solution is not just an effective way of learning about problems in ill-structured domains but also a good simulation of what happens in real-life business situations.

7.3. Learning by interacting through technology

Pen and paper have their merits as tools for cognitive support: they are portable, flexible, inexpensive and familiar. However, their limitations are increasingly apparent in the age of lightweight connected devices: they have a very small capacity for massive storage of data, they do not allow distance collaboration and they are mostly limited to letters, numbers, doodles and static images.

The blank screen of a connected laptop computer, tablet or smartphone, on the other hand, offers infinite possibilities. One can instantly access a Wikipedia article about a poorly understood concept. One can create a collaborative table that can be instantly filled with inputs from the other members of a small team or a large classroom. One may open a videoconferencing application that will instantly break all barriers of time and space, connecting students, teachers and guest speakers. One moment a student is using a Web-based interface to participate in a simulation, the next moment he or she is writing a spell-checked report, then he or she watches an online video from a prestigious university about any topic he or she fancies.

Technology is not a panacea that will revolutionize education, as some may claim. Ultimately, it is the critical and creative thinking of the technology user that will make the difference between a rich learning environment and a sterile series of easily accessible "infotainment" contents. Critical and creative thinking can be amplified through the use of collaborative connected tools, but it takes an experienced teacher to design an engaging course, suggest relevant contents and guide students through the process of developing their own intellectual autonomy. Garry Kasparov, the famous chess grand master and world champion, once stated that there is only one adversary capable of beating artificial intelligence chess players: a human–machine partnership that he calls centaurs. Like the mythical creatures that are half human and half horse, effective managers are becoming increasingly more competent at combining the creative spirit of the human mind with the horsepower of Big Data, artificial intelligence and collaborative networks. A good learning environment must emulate this cognitive partnership.

7.4. Learning by exploring the ecosystem

One of the great insights from Terra's treatment of McKinsey's 7S framework was adding the dimension "learning with the external environment" to the original model. Indeed, as discussed in Chapter 6, strategies, structures, systems and cultures must constantly be adapted according to an ever changing technological, socio-cultural and economic environment. Startups, scale-ups and large businesses alike must constantly monitor external sources of learning if they are to become or remain innovative. The main sources of innovation opportunities are well synthesized by the Quintuple Helix framework discussed above.

The same can be said about the learning process of entrepreneurship and innovation students. They should not be confined to the classroom walls, but they must be encouraged to visit innovation clusters, incubators, fab-labs and technology parks. Inviting external speakers to talk about their experience, their methods and tools is also necessary. Finally, students must be encouraged to develop networking skills from early on, feeding their LinkedIn profile with relevant content and proactively trying to grow their number of contacts with relevant stakeholders at local, national and international levels.

7.5. From idea to market: innovative business development frameworks

This book is designed to be a brief overview of the myriad tools and frameworks available to entrepreneurs and intrapreneurs in their innovation journey. It does not seek to be an exhaustive compilation of all the tools available, which would have been impossible. Rather, it strives to present a few essential tools that could help students and teachers of entrepreneurship and innovation to evolve from vague ideas to go-to-market strategies. As a brief recap of this trajectory, this final section summarizes this process, listing all the tools used (see Appendix 1 for a full list containing all the frameworks).

Chapter 1 dealt with the differences between management, entrepreneurship and innovation education. It also presented an overview of the entrepreneurial ecosystem surrounding the university–enterprise interface and the Quintuple Helix framework for understanding the impact of entrepreneurial, human, political, social and ecological capitals on the long-term sustainable development of startups. It investigated the ontological and educational levels of entrepreneurship education and its three objectives: raising awareness, developing skills and providing support to entrepreneurial projects. A framework based on strategic, pedagogical and operational enablers was proposed. Finally, we discussed the triangular concept of Collaborative Interactivity, which we applied throughout the book: reflection based on authentic situations, peer collaboration and technology-enhanced interactivity.

In Chapter 2, we focused on the progression from emergent to central to complementary visions using Filion's visionary model (1991). We saw that without a deep understanding of one's self drivers and abilities, on the one hand, and a deep knowledge of the market and its stakeholders, on the other hand, it is unlikely that the vision will develop into a successful new venture. We also saw that lead users (enthusiasts who are so passionate about a knowledge domain that they create solutions to their own problems in that domain before they are commercially available) are an important source of innovation in both entrepreneurial and intrapreneurial projects.

Chapter 3 presented all the basic components of a traditional business plan. We discussed the notion that business plans are a static appreciation of certain variables affecting the project in its early phases. As such, it is filled with dangerous biases and wishful thinking that could lead entrepreneurs to underestimate the complexity of the challenges they will face. We argued that the more dynamic approaches of business modeling and design thinking were much more adapted to innovative business evolution. In spite of these limitations, we defended the use of business plans in entrepreneurship and innovation education as a valid exercise that could help students understand the internal strengths and external opportunities, facilitating the development of the vision through better knowledge of the market. As long as its limitations are emphasized and more advanced tools are used to overcome its limitations, business plans can be an integral part of an entrepreneur's toolbox. In this chapter, we also discussed the following: how to structure a literature review in a business plan; how to conduct a market analysis; how to scan the PESTEL environment for political, economic, socio-cultural, technological, ecological and legal opportunities and threats; how to use Porter's Five Forces framework to understand the threats from rivals; how to establish a segmentation, targeting and positioning strategy based on the understanding of these opportunities and threats; how to develop the marketing mix for products and services; how to diagnose internal strengths and weaknesses using McKinsey's 7S framework; and Porter's Value Chain model. Finally, we discussed how the most relevant external and internal forces can lead to offensive and defensive strategies using the TOWS matrix. In the final section, we recommended that teachers use peer-to-peer approaches to facilitate Collaborative Interactivity principles of learning how to develop business plans.

In Chapter 4, we discussed how business modeling addresses the essential question of how value is created, delivered and captured in both new ventures and mature businesses. The Business Model Canvas was presented as a visual tool that facilitated discussion, communication and development of value strategies. The relationships between the nine building blocks of the model were highlighted using an ontology chart of the value flow in the canvas. We saw how earlier attempts at describing this value flow included McKinsey's value delivery system. The advantage of the BMC, as explained, is its ability to integrate both the right side of the process (value delivery and value capture) and its left side (value creation). The right side of the BMC was shown to be merely a visual representation of the age-old framework of marketing mix (7Ps). We showed how using a color code could help readers of BMCs more easily understand the different value flows involved. We compared Tidd's innovation wheel with the four types of innovation facilitated by business model design: offer-driven, customer-driven, resource-driven and finance-driven innovations. At the end of this chapter, we discussed how Osterwalder's BMC approach is part of a larger movement for dynamic business development known as the effectuation process. This process consists of constantly adapting one's means and goals based on the changes in the environment and the constraints they impose. As a synthesis, we argued that the BMC has become one of the most popular tools for implementing effectuation strategies because it helps users visualize the interactions among the nine value-creating dimensions while answering four key questions about their strategy: Is it feasible (from the perspective of resources)? Is it desirable (from the perspective of targeted customers)? Is it viable (from the perspective of revenues and cash flow) and is it adaptable (from the perspective of the external opportunities and threats)? We closed the chapter with a proposition of Collaborative Interactivity principles to facilitate teaching and learning business model design.

Throughout Chapter 5, we explored how product development evolved from the stage-gate system, slow and management-centric, to the Customer Development Model, much more agile and customer-centric. The Design Thinking and Lean Startup approaches have developed similar principles into mainstream adoption, emphasizing the ability to constantly empathize with customers before building and testing prototypes or minimum viable products. We looked at the stages of the Design Thinking and Lean Startup cycles, and how they can be combined with the Design Sprint method promoted by Google Ventures. Finally, we saw examples of powerful online tools to create Customer Journey Maps, prototypes and tests. In the Collaborative Interactivity principles section, we described how an entrepreneurship or innovation class could be enriched using these tools.

In Chapter 6, we discussed some of the knowledge management challenges of scaling up new ventures or innovative projects. We illustrated a management system with its four key resources (human, information, financial and material resources) and the fundamental process of planning, allocating and controlling these resources. We revisited McKinsey's 7S framework and argued that Terra's (2001) version of this model was more adapted to understanding knowledge management challenges. We gave examples of several companies that have successfully scaled up thanks to their ability to adapt their strategy based on what they learned from the external environment, and how they successfully adapted their structure, HR policies, culture and systems to remain innovative. We saw the importance of controlling performance with multiple-dimension metrics using tools such as the Balanced Scorecard. We then returned to the Quintuple Helix framework as an appropriate guide to map and prioritize the stakeholders in any company's ecosystem. In the Collaborative Interactivity section, we discussed how a simple qualitative analysis tool can be collaboratively built by students based on interviews with startup CEOs to synthesize common challenges they face when scaling up their operations while remaining innovative.

This book has listed more than 50 tools and frameworks that teachers and students of entrepreneurship and innovation can use both in the classroom and in "real-life" projects. It does not have the pretension of being exhaustive about any of the subjects covered, having preferred a horizontal overview of the proverbial "forest" rather than a vertical analysis of just a few "trees". We hope to have achieved the goal of sharing with people interested in E&I education a comprehensive toolbox to deal with different problems that emerge during this ambiguous and ill-structured adventure of creating startups or developing innovation projects.

Appendices

Appendix 1

List of Tools and Frameworks Used in the Book

Chapter 1. E&I Education: An Overview

– Differences between management and entrepreneurship education curricula

– Differences between entrepreneurship education and training targets

– University–Enterprise Interface and the entrepreneurial ecosystem

– The quintuple Helix model of sustainable development

– Key issues in entrepreneurship and innovation education: ontological and educational levels

– The triple objective of entrepreneurship programs: to raise awareness, develop skills and provide support

– The triple enablers: strategic, pedagogical and operational facilitators

– Collaborative interactivity as a pedagogical principle to entrepreneurship and innovation education

Chapter 2. From Idea to Vision

– Progression from emergent to central to complementary visions

– Relationship between elements supporting the entrepreneur's visionary process

– Lead users develop a solution to a deeply felt need before it is commercially available

Chapter 3. From Vision to Business Plan

– Elements of a funnel-like literature review structure

– Market analysis: from the marketing environment to the marketing mix

– The Political, Economic, Socio-Cultural, Technological, Environmental, Legal and Competitive external environment framework

– Porter's extended rivalry model

– Segmentation–targeting–positioning process

– Segmentation table with typical consumer segmentation criteria

– Perceptual map

– The 4Ps of product marketing and 3Ps of service marketing

– McKinsey's 7S framework

– Value Chain model

– TOWS matrix with offensive and defensive strategies

– Example of Google Docs shared sheet for peer-review dashboard

Chapter 4. From Business Plan to Business Model

– The Business Model Canvas

– Claimed benefits of business model artifacts

– Value flow in the ontology diagram of the Business Model Canvas

– Value Delivery System

– Iterative approach between the value creation and value delivery sides of the BMC

– Equivalence between the 7P framework and the right side of the BMC

– An example of color-coded multiple-sided business model

– Tidd and Bessant's Innovation Wheel

– Adoption rate of disruptive innovations

– Tidd's 4Ps associated with Osterwalder's innovation typology

– The effectuation process

– Four key questions to ask about any innovation opportunity

– Collaborative dashboard to create multiple-role teams for innovation project

Chapter 5. From Business Model Design to Design Thinking and Lean Startup

– The stage-gate system

– The Customer Development Model

– Design Thinking and Lean Startup approaches to innovation

– Traditional organizational learning and innovation

– Learning in an organization embedded with DT principles

– Design Thinking stages

– Lean Startup cycle

– Simplified Design Sprint Stages

– Example of CJM

Chapter 6. Scaling Up: The Challenges of Knowledge Management

– The "DNA" of management problems

– Illustration of a management system

– Revisiting the McKinsey's 7S framework

– The seven dimensions of knowledge management

– The Balanced Scorecard

– Revisiting the Quintuple Helix of knowledge flow in innovation ecosystems

– Stakeholder priority mapping

– Vertical and horizontal table for qualitative data analysis and synthesis

Appendix 2

Framework for Evaluating the Effectiveness of Entrepreneurship Teaching

This section reproduces the questionnaire used to create the framework discussed in Chapter 1 (the questionnaire is available online at https://goo.gl/fLR3nW).

This questionnaire is part of an ongoing research on the key enablers of entrepreneurial intent among higher education students. Your answers will be treated completely anonymously. There are three parts to this questionnaire: Strategic Enablers (3 questions), Pedagogical Enablers (8 questions) and Operational Enablers (3 questions). It should take you less than six minutes to complete. Thank you for your participation!

– What is the name of your University/Higher Education Institution?

– In which country is your University/HEI located?

– What is your profile?

Part 1 – Strategic Enablers

– Please answer each question on a scale of 1 (entirely disagree) to 5 (entirely agree) based on your experience of the entrepreneurial practices at your University/Higher Education Institution (HEI).

– SE1 – ICP – The entrepreneurship curriculum is constructed based on an ample consultation of all stakeholders involved (students, faculty, staff).

– SE2 – TTP – There are regular programs for training entrepreneurship teachers.

– SE3 – SPE – Our entrepreneurship activities are designed with student expectations and needs in mind.

Part 2 – Pedagogical Enablers

– Please answer each question on a scale of 1 (entirely disagree) to 5 (entirely agree) based on your experience of the entrepreneurial practices at your University/Higher Education Institution (HEI).

– PE1 – API – Teachers use innovative tools that encourage active participation of students, such as cases, simulations and role-playing games.

– PE2 – CAC – Teachers promote transversal competitions and challenges internally and encourage participation in external events.

– PE3 – DMA – There is an active effort among teachers to deconstruct myths and assumptions about new venture creation and becoming an entrepreneur.

– PE4 – SPD – Part of the curriculum is specifically designed to develop the sense of self-esteem and personal development among the students.

– PE5 – EMS – An effectuation mindset is encouraged, that is, students are taught to deal with the uncertainty and ambiguity of a complex environment rather than relying on the false sense of security of business plan predictions.

– PE6 – LRC – Students are inspired by the trajectory of local entrepreneurs who seem relevant and accessible to them rather than being only exposed to "world-class" entrepreneurs like Mark Zuckerberg.

– PE7 – ESR – Teachers emphasize the importance of ethical questions when creating new ventures, as well as the positive and negative social impacts of innovation.

– PE8 – TMC – The curriculum includes transversal or multidisciplinary projects in which students are encouraged to work with people from different backgrounds.

Part 3 – Operational Enablers

– Please answer each question on a scale of 1 (entirely disagree) to 5 (entirely agree) based on your experience of the entrepreneurial practices at your University/Higher Education Institution (HEI).

– OE1 – HPN – Teachers and students are encouraged to create projects with the local entrepreneurship ecosystem (incubators, small businesses, agencies, networks) in order to gain more experience and learn by doing.

– OE2 – PLC – Your university/HEI has physical infrastructure where entrepreneurs and faculty can meet and develop their ideas, such as incubators, FabLabs and co-working facilities.

– OE3 – FSP – Your university/HEI facilitates contact with venture capitalists, angel investors, funding programs and crowdfunding platforms.

Appendix 3

Sources of Secondary Data

These databases were selected based on likely availability in business schools. The list was compiled from the following sources:

https://www.library.hbs.edu/Find/Databases

https://kcenter.skema.edu/find/find-and-guide

https://learning-center.hec.edu/Library/Where-to-find/Databases

Amadeus	Contains financial statement data as well as basic company and management information for public and private companies in Europe
BCC Research	Reports on major economic, scientific and technological developments in industrial, pharmaceutical and high technology worldwide
Business Source Complete	Articles from academic journals, magazines and trade publications, as well as current company, industry and region reports
Business Source Ultimate (BSU)	Academic articles – Market analyses – Company profiles – Country profiles
Dalloz	Law – Jurisprudence
EconBiz	It is a subject portal for economics and business studies with excellent European coverage
Emerald	Academic articles
Factiva	Press articles – International area – Trends – Trades articles – Company data
Financial Times Archive	Archive including all articles, advertisements and market listings published in Financial Times from 1888 to 2016

Freedom Collection (Science Direct)	Academic articles
Google Scholar	Access to millions of academic sources with number of citations and full references
IMF eLibrary	Statistical data and reports from the International Monetary Fund
JSTOR	Scanned images of journal issues and pages, often dating back to the original issue
JSTOR	Academic articles
MarketResearch.com	Reports from market research firms covering health care, consumer goods, publishing, manufacturing and other markets and industries
Navis Fiscal	Law – Jurisprudence
OECD iLibrary	Country studies, forecasting publications, reports, periodicals and socio-economic databases from the Organisation for Economic Co-operation and Development
Orbis	Company data – Financial analyses
Proquest	Academic articles – Company data – Financial and Banking data
ProQuest Statistical Insight	Index to statistical content of government and private sector data sources
Scholarvox (Cyberlibris)	E-books
SciVal	Academic articles – Bibliometric studies
Scopus	Academic articles – Bibliometric studies
Statista	It is a searchable database of statistics, studies, dossiers, infographics and more
Web of Science	Provides complete bibliographic data plus citations and abstracts to journal articles across a wide range of scientific and technological disciplines
World DataBank	Central repository of data from the World Bank and sub-organizations
World Development Indicators	Statistics from the World Bank for almost 600 development indicators, dating as far back as 1960
Xerfi Knowledge	Market studies – Industry analyses – Company analyses – Economic news

Appendix 4

Franco-Russian Research Project on the Perceived Relevance of Design Thinking Education[1]

As the design thinking (DT) approach becomes more widespread not only among startups, but also among mature companies, demand for DT as a discipline has increased in business education. The integration of design thinking requires not only skilled employees familiar with its principles, but also significant changes in the management system and corporate culture. In order to assess the perceived relevance of DT in France and Russia, French business school SKEMA partnered with the Russian Foreign Trade Academy (RFTA) to implement an international research project involving 180 students (55% Russian and 45% French). All students were working as interns or apprentices (involving 105 companies). All respondents had a formal training in DT principles and were thus in a unique position to observe how these principles were applied in the companies they worked for.

The sample mainly consisted of large companies operating in various industries, such as luxury, technology, biotechnology and energy. A common online questionnaire was used as a research tool in France and Russia. The main topics were the perceived relevance of DT in the activities of the firm and the perceived effectiveness of this approach in various functional domains.

1 This project is part of the Franco-Russian University cooperation project involving Skema Business School, the Russian Foreign Trade Academy and several other institutions from both countries. These results were originally published by Komarova and Lima (2020).

The results obtained in the two countries are surprisingly homogeneous. Most of the study participants (87% of French respondents and 84% of Russian respondents) acknowledged the relevance and importance of DT skills for the professional activities of modern managers and specialists from various sectors of the economy (Figure A4.1).

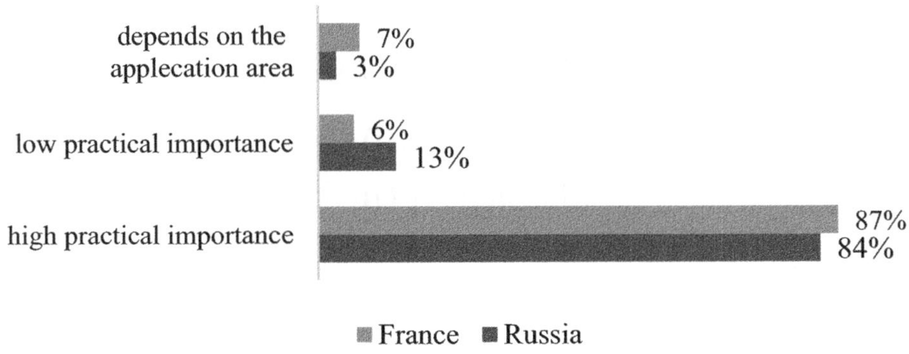

Figure A4.1. *The relevance of DT skills*

French and Russian participants were also unanimous in identifying three key areas where DT tools are mostly used (Figure A4.2): development of new products and services; optimization of business processes of the company and strategic and tactical planning.

Figure A4.2. *Areas of DT application*

More than half of the survey participants from Russia (61% of respondents) noted that DT tools are the domain of skilled specialists (Figure A4.3), whereas 45% of the French saw these tools being used at the level of structural units (45%). Very few respondents (2% and 4%) in both countries observed DT approaches being used at the corporate level.

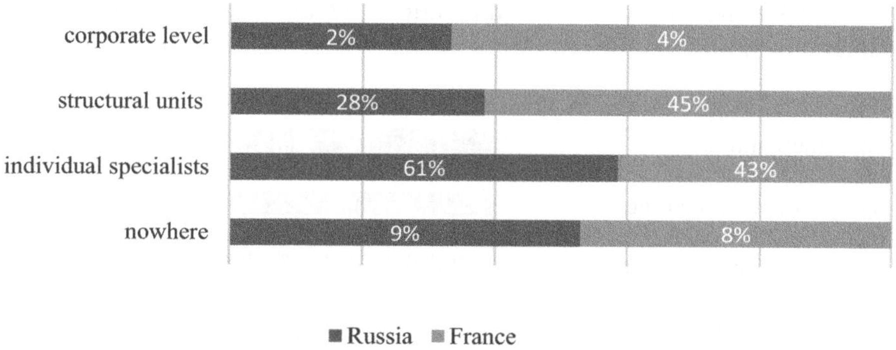

Figure A4.3. *Level of DT method application in companies*

The three main barriers to the effective use of DT at the corporate level identified by the survey participants were lack of time required to go through all stages of DT, insufficient level of knowledge and skills of employees in this area and the need to change the corporate culture and adapt it to the use of flexible management approaches (Figure A4.4).

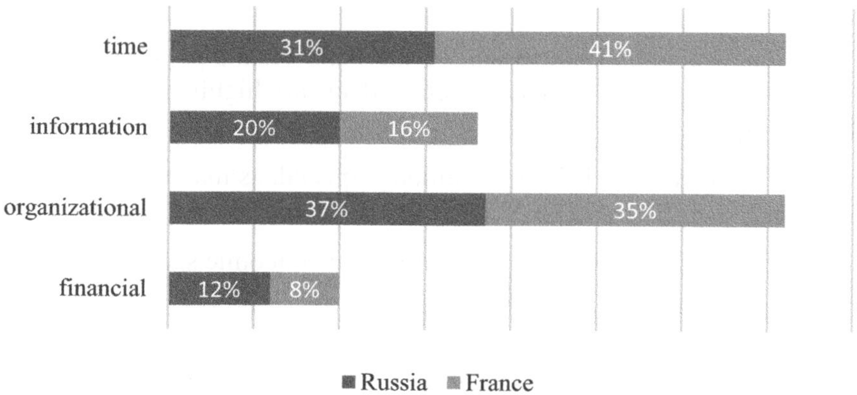

Figure A4.4. *Obstacles to DT application at the corporate level*

Concerning the domains in which DT is perceived to have the greatest effectiveness, Russian and French students disagreed slightly. For the Russians, DT is most effectively used to develop the creative thinking skills of employees (83%), cooperation with like-minded partners (69%) and developing new products and services (66%). The French saw the latter as the most important benefit of using DT (75%), followed by creativity (62%), with equally high rankings for motivation (52%), cooperation (53%) and adaptation (51%).

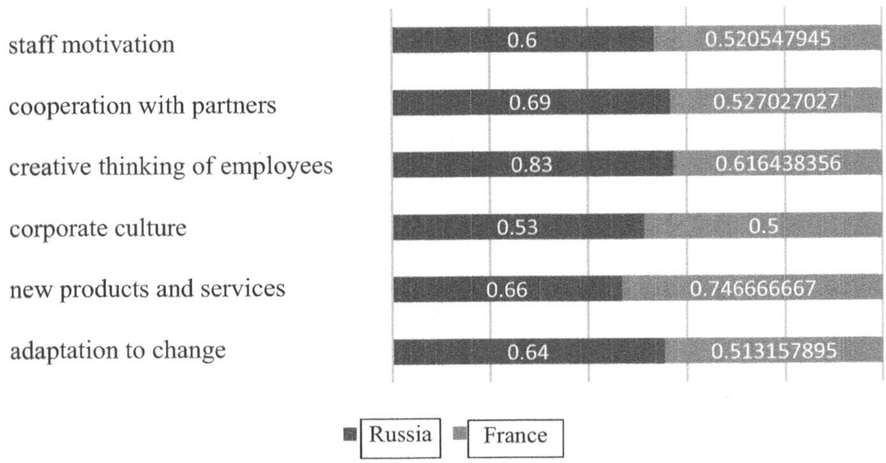

Figure A4.5. *Assessment of the potential effectiveness of the use of DT in companies*

Thus, cross-country comparison of the main results of the study shows that the answers of Russian and French students are highly convergent in the following aspects:

– High demand for DT skills among specialists/managers of modern companies.

– Perceived effectiveness of DT in different economic sectors.

– Cross-functional use of DT principles.

However, it should be noted that, in most modern companies, DT is not yet used at the corporate level. The fragmented/localized use of the DT seems to be common in both countries. The reason for this lies in the fact that the successful implementation of DT requires certain changes in the corporate culture, personnel management, organizational structure, and business processes and business communications. These factors are perceived as the main barriers to the effective implementation of DT in these companies. This study has confirmed the importance of reinforcing DT education in business and engineering schools in France and Russia. As evidence from the literature shows, companies that generalize the adoption of these principles are likely to become more creative, flexible and competitive.

References

Abdelkafi, N., Makhotin, S., and Posselt, T. (2013). Business model innovations for electric mobility – What can be learned from existing business model patterns? *International Journal of Innovation Management*, 17(1), 1–41.

Akola, E. and Heinonen, J. (2006). How to support learning of entrepreneurs? A study of training programmes for entrepreneurs in five European countries. *Proceedings of RENT XX Conference, Research in Entrepreneurship and Small Business*, Brussels, November 22–24.

Albertini, T., Fabiani, T., Lameta, N., and Lima, M. (2019). A framework for evaluating the effectiveness of entrepreneurial teaching in higher education. *Marché et Organisations*, 34(1), 159.

Alis, D., Dumas M., Le Goff, H., and Le Rudulier, K. (2014). L'impact de formations universitaires en entrepreneuriat sur le sentiment d'auto-efficacité, l'estime de soi et l'intention entrepreneuriale des étudiants : une étude longitudinale quantitative auprès de 225 étudiants. *Forum La Semaine du Management*, Université Aix Marseille, May.

Aouni, Z. (2011). Démystification d'une pédagogie émergente : l'approche par les compétences. *Entreprendre, Innover*, 3(11–12), 120–126

Appelo, J. (2020). Combining design thinking, lean startup, and agile development – Everyone misses the point of continuous innovation. *Shiftup* [Online]. Available: https://shiftup.work/combining-design-thinking-lean-startup-and-agile-development-everyone-misses-the-point-of-continuous-innovation/.

Appio, F.P., Lima, M., and Paroutis, S. (2019). Understanding smart cities: Innovation ecosystems, technological advancements, and societal challenges. *Technological Forecasting and Social Change*, 142, 1–14.

Arlotto, J., Boissin, J.P., and Maurin, S. (2011). L'intention entrepreneuriale des étudiants, grandes ecoles/universités : un faux débat? *5ème Congrès International de l'Académie de l'Entrepreneuriat.*

Arlotto, J., Jourdan, P., Sahut, J.M., and Teulon, F. (2012). Les programmes de formation à l'entrepreneuriat sont-ils réellement utiles ? Le cas des concours pédagogiques de création d'entreprise. *Management et avenir*, 5(55), 291–309.

Barès, F., Houe, T., and Jacquot, T. (2011). Le projet "junior-entreprise" comme outil pertinent d'initiation à l'entrepreneuriat : une analyse des comportements et compétences. *Revue de l'Entrepreneuriat*, 10(2), 89–119.

Barney, J., Wright, M., and Ketchen Jr, D.J. (2001). The resource-based view of the firm: Ten years after 1991. *Journal of Management*, 27(6), 625–641.

Bechard, J.P. and Gregoire, D. (2009). Archétypes d'innovations pédagogiques dans l'enseignement supérieur de l'entrepreneuriat : modèle et illustrations. *Revue de l'Entrepreneuriat*, 8(2), 35–56.

Bennett R. (2006). Business lecturers' perceptions of the nature of entrepreneurship. *International Journal of Entrepreneurial Behavior, Research*, 12, 165–188.

Berlo, D.K. (1999). *O Processo de Comunicação: Introdução à Teoria e à Prática*. São Paulo Martins Fontes Editora, São Paulo.

Blank, S. (2013), Why the lean start-up changes everything. *Harvard Business Review*, 91(5), 63–72.

Blank, S. (2020). *The Four Steps to the Epiphany: Successful Strategies for Products that Win*. John Wiley & Sons, Hoboken, NJ.

Boissin, J.P. and Schieb-Bienfait, N. (2011). Des maisons de l'entrepreneuriat au plan d'action national des pôles entrepreneuriat étudiants. *Entreprendre, Innover*, 3(11–12), 55–64.

Boissin, J.P., Chollet B., and Emin, S. (2007). Les croyances des étudiants envers la création d'entreprise. Un état des lieux. *Revue Française de Gestion*, 11(180), 25–43.

Boissin, J.P., Chollet, B., and Emin, S. (2009). Les déterminants de l'intention de créer une entreprise chez les étudiants : un test empirique. *M@an@gement*, 12(1), 28–51.

Bouwman, H., Haaker, T., and De Vos, H. (2008). *Mobile Service Innovation and Business Models*. Springer, New York, NY.

Brand, S., Blosch, M., and Osmond, N. (2019). Enterprise architects combine design thinking, lean startup and agile to drive digital innovation. *Gartner Report* [Online]. Available: https://www.gartner.com/en/documents/3941917/enterprise-architects-combine-design-thinking-lean-start.

Brown, T. and Katz, B. (2019). *Change by Design: How Design Thinking Transforms Organizations and Inspires Innovation*. Harper Business, New York, NY.

Bureau, S. and Fendt J. (2012). La dérive “situationniste”. Le plus court chemin pour apprendre à entreprendre ? *Revue Française de Gestion*, 4(233), 181–200.

Carayannis, E.G., Barth, T.D., and Campbell, D.F. (2012). The quintuple helix innovation model: Global warming as a challenge and driver for innovation. *Journal of Innovation and Entrepreneurship*, 1(1), 2.

Carrier, C. (2009). L’enseignement de l’entrepreneuriat au delà des cours magistraux, des études de cas et du plan d’affaires ? *Revue de l’Entrepreneuriat*, 8(2), 17–33.

Cavalcante, S. (2014). Designing business model change. *International Journal of Innovation Management*, 18(2), 1–22.

Chambard, O. (2013). La promotion de l’entrepreneuriat dans l’enseignement supérieur. Les enjeux d’une création lexicale. *Mots. Les Langages du Politique*, (102), 103–119.

Chené, E., Schieb-Bienfait, N., Lavergne, A., and Tregret-Bouche, I. (2011). Une démarche de conception d’un dispositif de sensibilisation à l’entrepreneuriat. *Annales des Mines – Gérer et Comprendre*, (103), 60–70.

Chesbrough, H. (2003). *Open Innovation: The New Imperative for Creating and Profiting from Technology*. Harvard Business School Press, Boston, MA.

Chesbrough, H. (2010), Business model innovation: Opportunities and barriers. *Long Range Planning*, 43(2), 354–363.

Chesbrough, H. and Rosenbloom, R. (2002). The role of the business model in capturing value from innovation: Evidence from Xerox Corporation’s technology spin-off companies. *Industrial and Corporate Change*, 11(3), 529–555.

Christensen, C. (1997). *The Innovator’s Dilemma: When New Technologies Cause Great Firms to Fail*. Harvard Business Review Press, Boston, MA.

Christensen C., Anthony D., and Roth E. (2004). *Seeing What’s Next. Using the Theories of Innovation to Predict Industry Change*. Harvard Business School Press, Boston, MA.

Clark, B.R. (1998). *Creating Entrepreneurial Universities: Organisational Pathways of Transformation. Issues in Hihger Education*. Pergamon Press for International Association of Universities, Oxford.

Cooper, R.G. (1990). Stage-gate systems: A new tool for managing new products. *Business Horizons*, 33(3), 44–54.

Cooper, R.G. (2014). What's next? After stage-gate. *Research-Technology Management*, 57(1), 20–31.

Cringely, R.X. (1996). *Accidental Empires: How the Boys of Silicon Valley Make their Millions, Battle Foreign Competition, and Still Can't Get a Date*. Basic Books, New York, NY.

Davenport, T.H. (2013). *Process Innovation: Reengineering Work through Information Technology*. Harvard Business Press, Boston, MA.

Degeorge, J.M. and Fayolle, A. (2011). Les étudiants français ont-ils la fibre entrepreneuriale ? *Entreprendre et Innover*, 1(9–10), 21–28.

De Reuver, M., Bouwman, H., and Haaker, T. (2013). Business model roadmapping: A practical approach to come from an existing to a desired business model. *International Journal of Innovation Management*, 17(1), 1–18.

Dervaux, C. (2011). Vis ma vie et découvre mon entreprise. *Entreprendre, Innover*, 3(11–12), 95–102.

Dew, N., Read, S., Sarasvathy, S.D., and Wiltbank, R. (2009). Effectual versus predictive logics in entrepreneurial decision-making: Differences between experts and novices. *Journal of Business Venturing*, 24, 287–309.

Dodd, S.D., Jack, S., and Anderson, A.R. (2013). From admiration to abhorrence: The contentious appeal of entrepreneurship across Europe. *Entrepreneurship, Regional Development*, 25(1–2), 69–89.

Drucker, P.F. (1994). *Innovation and Entrepreneurship: Practice and Principles*. Heinemann, London.

Eppler, M., Hoffmann, F., and Bresciani, S. (2011). New business models through collaborative idea generation. *International Journal of Innovation Management*, 15(06), 1323–1341.

Etzkowitz, H. and Leydesdorff, L. (2000). The dynamics of innovation: From national systems and "mode 2" to a triple helix of university-industry-government relations. *Research Policy*, 29, 109–123.

Euchner, J. and Ganguly, A. (2014). Business model innovation in practice. *Research Technology Management*, 57(6), 33–39.

Fayolle, A. (2012). *Entrepreneuriat, Apprendre à Entreprendre*, 2nd edition. Dunod, Paris.

Fayolle, A. and Gailly, B. (2008). From craft to science: Teaching models and learning processes in entrepreneurship education. *Journal of European Industrial Training*, 32(7), 569–593.

Fayolle, A. and Gailly B. (2009). Evaluation d'une formation en entrepreneuriat : prédisposition et impact sur l'intention d'entreprendre. *M@n@gement*, 12(3), 176–203.

Fayolle, A. and Toutain, O. (2013). Four educational principles to rethink ethically entrepreneurship education. *Revista de Economia Mundial*, (35), 21–45.

Fayolle, A. and Verzat C. (2009). Pédagogies actives et entrepreneuriat : quelle place dans nos enseignements ? *Revue de l'Entrepreneuriat*, 8(2), 1–16.

Fielt, E. (2014). Conceptualising business models: Definitions, frameworks and classifications. *Journal of Business Models*, 1(1), 85–105.

Fiet, J.O. (2001). The theoretical side of teaching entrepreneurship. *Journal of Business Venturing*, 16(1), 1–24.

Filion, L.J. (1991). *Visions et relations : clés du succès de l'entrepreneur*. Les éditions de l'entrepreneur, Montreal.

Filion, L.J., Schmitt, C., and Ananou, C. (2012). *Réussir sa création d'entreprise sans business plan : en construisant son opportunité, en travaillant son intuition, avec les approches IDEO et SynOpp*. Editions Eyrolles, Saint-Germain.

Freiberger, P. and Swaine, M. (1999). *Fire in the Valley: The Making of the Personal Computer*. McGraw-Hill Professional, New York, NY.

Fritscher, B. and Pigneur, Y. (2010). Supporting business model modelling: A compromise between creativity and constraints. In *Task Models and Diagrams for User Interface Design*, England, D., Palanque, P., Vanderdonckt, J., Wild, P.J. (eds). Springer, Berlin, Heidelberg.

Futterer, F., Jochen, S., and Heidenreich, S. (2018). Effectuation or causation as the key to corporate venture success? Investigating effects of entrepreneurial behaviors on business model innovation and venture performance. *Long Range Planning*, 51(1), 64–81.

GEM (2014). Global Entrepreneurship Monitor Survey [Online]. Available: http://www.gemconsortium.org/report.

Granovetter, M.S. (1973). The strength of weak ties. *American Journal of Sociology*, 78(6), 1360–1380.

Greer, J., McCalla, G.I., Cooke, J.E., Collins, J.A., Kumar, V.S., Bishop, A.S., and Vassileva, J.I. (2000). Integrating cognitive tools for peer help: The intelligent intranet peer help-desk project. *Computers as Cognitive Tools*, 2, 69–96.

Grönlund, J., Sjödin, D.R., and Frishammar, J. (2010). Open innovation and the stage-gate process: A revised model for new product development. *California Management Review*, 52(3), 106–131.

Günzel, F. and Holm, A. (2013). One size does not fit all – understanding the front-end and back-end of business model innovation. *International Journal of Innovation Management*, 17(1), 1–34.

Hallam, C., Zanella, G., Dorantes Dosamantes, C.A., and Cardenas, C. (2016). Measuring entrepreneurial intent? Temporal construal theory shows it depends on your timing. *International Journal of Entrepreneurial Behavior, Research*, 22(5), 671–697.

Handy, C. (1993). *Understanding Organizations*. Penguin, UK.

Henrekson, M. and Sanandaji, T. (2018). Schumpeterian entrepreneurship in Europe compared to other industrialized regions. *International Review of Entrepreneurship*, 16(2), 157–182.

Hills, G.E. (1988). Variations in university entrepreneurship education: An empirical study of an evolving field. *Journal of Business Venturing*, 3(2), 109–122.

Hindle, K. (2007). Teaching entrepreneurship at the university: From the wrong building to the right philosophy. In *Handbook of Research in Entrepreneurship Education*, Edward Elgar Publishing, Aldershot.

Hofer, A. (2010). From strategy to practice in university entrepreneurship support: Strengthening entrepreneurship and local economic development in eastern germany: Youth, entrepreneurship and innovation. Working paper, OECD Local Economic and Employment Development (LEED), 09.

Holiday, R. (2014). *Growth Hacker Marketing: A Primer on the Future of PR, Marketing, and Advertising*. Penguin, UK.

Ilgen, D.R., Hollenbeck, J.R., Johnson, M., and Jundt, D. (2005). Teams in organizations: From input-process-output models to IMOI models. *Annual Review of Psychology*, 56, 517–543.

Johnson, D. (2001). What is innovation and entrepreneurship? Lessons for large organizations. *Industrial and Commercial Training*, 33(4), 135–140.

Johnson, D., Craig, J.B.L., and Hildebrand, R. (2006). Entrepreneurship education: Towards a discipline-based framework. *Journal of Management Development*, 25, 40–54.

Johnson, M., Christensen, C., and Kagermann, H. (2008). Reinventing your business model. *Harvard Business Review*, 86(12), 50–59.

Jonassen, D.H., Peck, K.L., and Wilson, B.G. (1999). *Learning with Technology: A Constructivist Perspective*. Merrill, Upper Saddle River, NJ.

Jones, C., and Penaluna, A. (2013). Moving beyond the business plan in enterprise education. *Education and Training,* 55(8/9), 804–814.

Jouison, E. and Verstraete, T. (2008). Business model et création d'entreprise. *Revue Française de Gestion*, 29(1), 175–197.

Kaplan, R.S. and Norton, D.P. (1996). *The Balanced Scorecard: Translating Strategy Into Action*. Harvard Business Press, Boston, MA.

Kirzner, I.M. (1999). Creativity and/or alertness: A reconsideration of the Schumpeterian entrepreneur. *The Review of Austrian Economics*, 11(1–2), 5–17.

Kitagawa, F. (2005). Universités entrepreneuriales et développement régional. *Politique et Gestion de l'Enseignement Supérieur*, 5(17), 69–97.

Klapper, L., Amit, R., Guillen, M.F., and Quesada, J.M. (2010). Entrepreneurship and firm formation across countries. In *International Differences in Entrepreneurship*, Lerner, J. and Schoar, A. (eds). The University of Chicago Press, Chicago, IL.

Kline, S.J., Rosenberg, N., and Landau, R. (1986). The positive sum strategy: Harnessing technology for economic growth. *An Overview of Innovation*, 275–307.

Knapp, J., Zeratsky, J., and Margolis, M. (2016). *Sprint: How to Solve Big Problems and Test New Ideas in Just Five Days*. Simon & Schuster, New York, NY.

Komarova, A.V. and Lima, M. (2020). Design thinking in international business: Practice and trends of use in Russian and French companies. *Russian Foreign Economic Bulletin*, (2).

Lam, W. (2010). Funding gap, what funding gap? Financial bootstrapping. *International Journal of Entrepreneurial Behavior, Research*, 16(4), 268–295.

Lanning, M. and Michaels, E. (1988). A business is a value delivery system. Staff paper, McKinsey, London.

Laperche, B., Lima, M., Seuillet, E., and Trousse, B. (2019). *Ecosystèmes d'innovation : regards croisés des acteurs clés*. L'Harmattan, Paris.

Lautenschläger, A. and Haase, H. (2011). The myth of entrepreneurship education: Seven arguments against teaching business creation at universities. *Journal of Entrepreneurship Education*, 14(147), 149.

Lima, M. (2001). *Inserção de Um Agente Indutor da Relação Universidade – Empresa em Sistema de Inovação Fragmentado*. IEL-BA [Online]. Available at: https://doi.org/10.1590/S1415-65552001000200007.

Lima, M. (2003). Potencial de suporte cognitivo das tecnologias interativas de comunicação: desenvolvimento de uma Interface hipertextual dinâmica para análise organizacional baseada em estudos de casos. Doctoral Dissertation, UFBA, Salvador.

Lima, M. (2020). Smarter organizations: Insights from a smart city hybrid framework. *International Entrepreneurship and Management Journal*, 1–20.

Lima, M. and Baudier, P. (2017). Business model canvas acceptance among French entrepreneurship students: Principles for enhancing innovation artefacts in business education. *Journal of Innovation Economics and Management*, 2(23), 159–183.

Lima, M. and Dolabela, F. (2000). Entrepreneurship learning in Brazilian institutions of higher education. *4th International Conference on Technology Policy and Innovation*. Florianopolis.

Lima, M. and Fabiani, T. (2014). *Teaching With Cases: A Framework-based Approach*. Amazon Create Space, Scotts Valley, CA.

Lima, M. and Fabiani, T. (2016). *Réussir mes études de cas : outils et mises en situation, modèles analytiques, mini-cas d'entreprises*. Dunod, Paris.

Lima, M. and Hastenreiter, H. (2008). Challenges and opportunities in the creation of a sustainable technology park in an immature local system of innovation: The case of tecnovia, Brazil. *Triple Helix VII – 7th Biennal International Conference on University, Industry, Government Linkages*.

Lima, M., Koehler, M.J., and Spiro, R.J. (2004). Collaborative interactivity and integrated thinking in Brazilian business schools using cognitive flexibility hypertexts: The panteon project. *Journal of Educational Computing Research*, 31(4), 371–406.

Lima, M. and Nivet, B. (2015). *L'Entreprise et son environnement : entreprendre, apprendre, s'adapter*. Amazon CreateSpace, Scotts Valley, CA.

Lima, M. and Seulliet, E. (2019). Évolution des écosystèmes d'innovation : des origines de la métaphore écologique à une nouvelle génération. In *Les écosystèmes d'innovation : regards croisés des acteurs clés,* Laperche, B., Lima, M., Seulliet, E., Trousse, B. (eds). L'Harmattan, Paris.

Lima, M., Cabrol, C., Marchandé, N., and Hastenreiter, H. (2008). Defying conventional wisdom by creating technology parks in immature systems of innovation: The case of Sophia Antipolis and Tecno Via. *IFBAE*, Grenoble.

Lima, M., Fabiani, T., and Namaci, L. (2014). A netnographic study of entrepreneurial traits: Evaluating classic typologies using the crowdsourcing algorithm of an online community. *Independent Journal of Management & Production*, 5(3), 693–709.

Lima, M., Baudier, P., and Boufaden, N. (2018). Perception de l'usabilité des outils d'innovation : le biais du genre dans l'utilisation du business model canvas. *Innovations : Revue d'Économie et de Management de l'Innovation*, 3(57), 59–84.

Lima, M., Baudier, P., Alawamleh, K., and Seguin, B. (2020). Motivations intrinsèques et extrinsèques des utilisateurs de systèmes de covoiturage. *Technologie et Innovation*, 5(1).

Link, P. and Lewrick, M. (2014). Agile methods in a new area of innovation management. *Science-to-Business Marketing Conference*, June, 3–4.

Loue, C., Laviolette E.M., and Bonnafous-Boucher M. (2008). L'entrepreneur à l'épreuve de ses compétences : éléments de construction d'un référentiel en situation d'incubation. *Revue de l'Entrepreneuriat*, 7, 63–83.

Lucena, C. and Fuks, H. (2000). *A Educação na Era da Internet: Professores e Aprendizes na Web*. Clube do Futuro, Rio de Janeiro.

Marchesnay, M., Chabchoub Kammoun S., and Ellouze Karray H. (2006). Y-a-t-il un entrepreneuriat méditerranéen ? *Revue Française de Gestion*, 32(166), 101–118.

Matta, A. (2001). Procedimentos de autoria hipermídia em redes de computadores: um ambiente mediador para o ensino-aprendizagem de história. Doctoral Thesis, Programa de Pós-Graduação em Educação, Faculdade de Educação – UFBA., Salvador.

Maurya, A. (2012). *Running Lean: Iterate from Plan A to a Plan that Works*. O'Reilly Media, Sebastopol, CA.

Mendelow, A.L. (1981). Environmental scanning-the impact of the stakeholder concept. *ICIS – International Conference on Information Systems Proceedings*, 20.

Mintzberg, H. (1989). *Mintzberg on Management, Inside Our Strange World of Organizations*. The Free Press, New York, NY.

Mueller, S. (2011). Increasing entrepreneurial intention: Effective entrepreneurship course characteristics. *International Journal of Entrepreneurship and Small Business*, 13(1), 55–74.

Müller, R.M. and Thoring, K. (2012). Design thinking vs. lean startup: A comparison of two user-driven innovation strategies, leading through design. *Proceedings of the DMI 2012 International Research Conference*, August 8–9, 2012 – Boston, MA.

Mullins, J.W. and Komisar, R. (2010). A business plan? Or a journey to plan B? *MIT Sloan Management Review*, 51(3), 1.

Mwasalwiba, E.S. (2010). Entrepreneurship education: A review of its objectives, teaching methods, and impact indicators. *Education and Training*, 52(1), 20–47.

Namaci, L., Lima, M., and Fabinani, T. (2013). De l'ombre à la lumière. Acquisition de connaissances, "Formalisation" de l'entrepreneuriat "Informel" dans les pays en voie de développement : cas du Maroc. *ICSB International Conference on Small Business*, Puerto Rico.

Nonaka, I. and Takeuchi, H. (1995). *The Knowledge Creating Company: How Japanese Companies Create the Dynamics of Innovation*. Oxford University Press, Oxford.

OECD (2005). *Oslo Manual: Guidelines for Collecting and Interpreting Innovation Data*. OECD Publisher, Paris.

Oosterbeek, H., Van Praag, M., and Ijsselstein, A. (2010). The impact of entrepreneurship education on entrepreneurship skills and motivation. *European Economic Review*, 54, 442–454.

Osterwalder, A. (2004). The business model ontology: A proposition in a design science approach. PhD Dissertation, Lausanne University, Lausanne.

Osterwalder, A. (2016). Why companies fail, how to prevent it. Strategyzer blog, June 20 [Online]. Available: https://www.strategyzer.com/blog/posts/2016/6/20/why-companies-fail-how-to-prevent-it.

Osterwalder, A. and Pigneur, Y. (2010). *Business Model Generation: A Handbook for Visionaries, Game Changers, and Challengers*. John Wiley & Sons, Hoboken, NJ.

Osterwalder, A. and Pigneur, Y. (2014). *Value Proposition Design*. John Wiley & Sons, Hoboken, NJ.

Osterwalder, A., Pigneur, Y., and Tucci, C. (2005). Clarifying business models: Origins, present, and future of the concept. *Communications of the Association for Information Systems*, 16(1), 1–25.

Paturel, R. and Arasti, Z. (2006). Les principaux déterminants de l'entrepreunariat féminin en Iran. *8ème Congrès International Francophone en Entrepreneuriat et PME*, 26–28 October, Fribourg.

Pittaway, L. and Cope, J. (2007). Entrepreneurship education: A systematic review of the evidence. *International Small Business Journal*, 25(5), 479–510.

Platje, A. and Wadman, S. (1998). From plan-do-check-action to PIDCAM: The further evolution of the Deming-wheel. *International Journal of Project Management*, 16(4), 201–208.

Porter, M. (1980). *Competitive Strategy: Techniques for Analyzing Industries and Competitors*. The Free Press, New York, NY.

Porter, M. (1985). *Competitive Advantage: Creating and Sustaining Superior Performance*. Simon & Schuster, New York, NY.

Porter, M. (1990). New global strategies for competitive advantage. *Planning Review*, 18(3), 4–14.

Pynnönen, M., Hallikas, J., and Ritala, P. (2012). Managing customer-driven business model innovation. *International Journal of Innovation Management*, 16(4), 1–18.

Rideout, E.C. and Gray, D.O. (2013). Does entrepreneurship education really work? A review and methodological critique of the empirical literature on the effects of university-based entrepreneurship education. *Journal of Small Business Management*, 51(3), 329–351.

Ries, E. (2011). *The Lean Startup: How Today's Entrepreneurs Use Continuous Innovation to Create Radically Successful Businesses*. Penguin, London.

Rinne, R. and Koivula, J. (2005). La place nouvelle de l'université et le choc des valeurs. *Revue Politique et Gestion de l'Enseignement Supérieur*, 3(17), 99–132.

Rodet-Kroichvili, N., Cabaret, K., and Picard, F. (2014). New insights into innovation: The business model approach and Chesbrough's seminal contribution to open innovation. *Journal of Innovation Economics & Management*, 15(3), 79–99.

Roegiers, X. (2012). Les institutions et leurs réformes de programme. In *Quelles réformes pédagogiques pour l'enseignement supérieur ?*, Roegiers, X., Miled, M., Ratziu, I., Letor, C., Etienne, R., Hubert, G., Dali, M. (eds). De Boeck, Brussels.

Sales-Wuillemin, E. (1991). De l'appréhension des significations implicites : verbes factifs et contrefactifs. *L'Année Psychologique*, 91(4), 559–580.

Samwel Mwasalwiba, E. (2010). Entrepreneurship education: A review of its objectives, teaching methods, and impact indicators. *Education and Training*, 52(1), 20–47.

Sarasvathy, S.D. (2001). Causation and effectuation: Toward a theorical shift from economic inevitability to entrepreneurial contingency. *The Academy of Management Review*, 26(2), 243–263.

Sarow, M.S. and Stuart, B.E. (2013). Teaching interdisciplinarity, creativity and innovation in business communication for a global marketplace. In *Creativity and Entrepreneurship: Changing Currents in Education and Public-life*, Book, L. and Phillips, D.P. (eds). Edward Elgard, Cheltenham.

Schneider, S. and Spieth, P. (2013). Business model innovation: Towards an integrated future research agenda. *International Journal of Innovation Management*, 17(1), 1–34.

Schneider, S. and Spieth, P. (2014). Business model innovation and strategic flexibility: Insights from an experimental research design. *International Journal of Innovation Management*, 18(6), 1–21.

Schumpeter, J.A. (1982). *The Theory of Economic Development: An Inquiry into Profits, Capital, Credit, Interest, and the Business Cycle (1912/1934)*. Transaction Publishers, New Jersey.

Selinger, M. (2001). Setting authentic tasks using the internet in schools. In *Issues in Teaching Using ICT*, Leask, M. (ed.). Routledge Falmer, London.

Shattock M. (2005). Les universités européennes et l'entrepreneuriat : leur rôle dans l'Europe du savoir. *Revue Politique et Gestion de l'Enseignement Supérieur*, 3(17), 12–26.

Singh, V.K. (2013). PDCA cycle: A quality approach. *Utthan – Journal of Management Sciences*, 1(1), 89–96.

Sommer, A.F., Hedegaard, C., Dukovska-Popovska, I., and Steger-Jensen, K. (2015). Improved product development performance through Agile/Stage-Gate hybrids: The next-generation Stage-Gate process? *Research-Technology Management*, 58(1), 34–45.

Stone, B. (2013). *The Everything Store: Jeff Bezos and the Age of Amazon*. Random House, Manhattan, NY.

Surlemont, B. and Kearney P. (2009). *Pédagogie et Esprit d'Entreprendre*. De Boeck, Brussels.

Teece, D. (2010). Business models, business strategy and innovation. *Long Range Planning*, 43(2), 172–194.

Ten Have, S., Ten Have, W., Stevens, F., and Van Der Elst, M. (2003). *Key Management Models: The Management Tools and Practices that Will Improve Your Business*. Prentice Hall, Upper Saddle River, NJ.

Tidd, J. and Bessant, J.R. (2013). *Managing Innovation: Integrating Technological, Market and Organizational Change*. John Wiley & Sons, Hoboken, NJ.

Terra, J.C.C. (2001). *Gestão do conhecimento: O grande desafio empresarial*. Negócio, São Paulo.

Tounes, A. (2006). L'intention entrepreneuriale des étudiants : le cas français. *La Revue des Sciences de Gestion*, 3(219), 57–65.

Toutain, O. (2011). La situation-problème pour construire ses connaissances entrepreneuriales. *Entreprendre et Innover*, 3(11–12), 127–136.

Toutain, O. and Salgado, M. (2015). Quels sont les effets des pédagogies actives dans l'apprentissage l'entrepreneuriat? Étude des changements de perceptions des élèves ingénieurs et managers à l'issue de la formation M.I.M.E. (Méthode d'Initiation au Métier d'Entrepreneur). *Revue de l'Entrepreneuriat*, 13(2), 55–88.

Toutain, O., Gaujard, C., Mueller, S., and Bornard, F. (2014). Dans quel Ecosystème Educatif Entrepreneurial vous retrouvez-vous ? *Entreprendre et Innover*, 4(23), 31–44.

Trimi, S. and Berbegal-Mirabent, J. (2012). Business model innovation in entrepreneurship. *International Entrepreneurship and Management Journal*, 8(4), 449–465.

Tushman, M. and O'Reilly, C. (1996). Ambidextrous organizations: Managing evolutionary and revolutionary change. *California Management Review*, 38(4), 8–30.

Valerio, A., Parton, B., and Robb, A. (2014). *Entrepreneurship Education and Training Programs around the World: Dimensions for Success*. The World Bank, Washington, D.C., WA.

Varela, R. and Jimenez, J.E. (2001). The effect of entrepreneurship education in the universities of Cali. *Frontiers of Entrepreneurship Research, Basbon Conference Proceedings*.

Venkatesh, V., Morris, M.G., Davis, G.B., and Davis, F.D. (2003). User acceptance of information technology: Toward a unified view. *MIS Quarterly*, 27(3), 425–478.

Venkatesh, V., Thong, J.Y., and Xu, X. (2012). Consumer acceptance and use of information technology: Extending the unified theory of acceptance and use of technology. *MIS Quarterly*, 36(1), 157–178.

Verstraete, T., Jouison-Laffitte, E., Kremer, F., Hlady Rispal, M., Boncler, J., Boucher, T., Bousquet, F., Dondi, J., Meiar, A., Papin, C., and Scipion, F. (2011). Recherche-action pour apprécier l'utilité du concept de Business Model pour les jeunes dirigeants d'entreprise du bâtiment, *Revue de l'Entrepreneuriat*, 11(4), 68–94.

Verstraete, T., Kremer, F., and Jouison-Laffitte, E. (2012), Le business model : une théorie pour des pratiques. *Entreprendre et Innover*, (1), 7–26.

Verzat, C. (2011). Expérimenter et coopérer pour apprendre à entreprendre. *Entreprendre et Innover*, 3(11–12), 113–119.

Verzat, C. and Garant, M. (2010). L'accompagnement dans les institutions d'enseignement supérieur. In *Accompagner des étudiants*, Raucent, B., Verzat, C., Villeneuve, L. De Boeck, Brussels.

Verzat, C. and Granger B. (2012). Accompagner plutôt qu'enseigner le business plan : bilan d'une expérimentation pédagogique. *Entreprendre et Innover*, 3(15), 40–49.

Von Hippel, E. (1988). *Sources of Innovation*. Oxford University Press, New York, NY.

Waterman Jr, R.H., Peters, T.J., and Phillips, J.R. (1980). Structure is not organization. *Business Horizons*, 23(3), 14–26.

Wilson, K.E. (2008). Entrepreneurship education in Europe. In *Entrepreneurship and Higher Education*. OECD Publishing, Paris.

Wright, M., Clarysse, B., Mustar, P., and Lockett, A. (2007). *Academic Entrepreneurship in Europe*. Edward Elgar Publishing, Cheltenham.

Yin, R.K. (2013). *Case Study Research: Design and Methods*. Sage Publications, Los Angeles, CA.

Young, M.F. (1995). Tecnología interactiva para la enseñanza: integración de una lección interactivaen videodisco con las actividades tradicionales de la clase. In *Nuevos Medios, Viejos Aprendizajes: Las Nuevas Tecnologías en la Educación*, Limon, A. (ed.). Universidad Iberoamericana, A.C., Mexico.

Zastempowski, M. and Przybylska, N. (2016). Cooperation in creating innovation in Polish small and medium-sized enterprises in the light of empirical studies. *Journal of Competitiveness*, 8, 42–58.

Zott, C. and Amit, R. (2007). Business model design and the performance of entrepreneurial firms. *Organization Science*, 18(2), 181–199.

Zott, C. and Amit, R. (2008). The fit between product market strategy and business model: Implications for firm performance. *Strategic Management Journal*, 29(1), 1–26.

Zott, C., Amit, R., and Massa, L. (2011). The business model: Recent developments and future research. *Journal of Management*, 37(4), 1019–1042.

Index

Other titles from

ISTE

in

Innovation, Entrepreneurship and Management

2020

ANDREOSSO-O'CALLAGHAN Bernadette, DZEVER Sam, JAUSSAUD Jacques, TAYLOR Robert
Sustainable Development and Energy Transition in Europe and Asia (Innovation and Technology Set – Volume 9)

BEN SLIMANE Sonia, M'HENNI Hatem
Entrepreneurship and Development: Realities and Future Prospects (Smart Innovation Set – Volume 30)

CHOUTEAU Marianne, FOREST Joëlle, NGUYEN Céline
Innovation for Society: The P.S.I. Approach (Smart Innovation Set – Volume 28)

CORON Clotilde
Quantifying Human Resources: Uses and Analysis (Technological Changes and Human Resources Set – Volume 2)

CORON Clotilde, GILBERT Patrick
Technological Change (Technological Changes and Human Resources Set – Volume 1)

CERDIN Jean-Luc, PERETTI Jean-Marie
The Success of Apprenticeships: Views of Stakeholders on Training and Learning
(Human Resources Management Set – Volume 3)

DELCHET-COCHET Karen
Circular Economy: From Waste Reduction to Value Creation
(Economic Growth Set – Volume 2)

DIDAY Edwin, GUAN Rong, SAPORTA Gilbert, WANG Huiwen
Advances in Data Science
(Big Data, Artificial Intelligence and Data Analysis Set – Volume 4)

DOS SANTOS PAULINO Victor
Innovation Trends in the Space Industry
(Smart Innovation Set – Volume 25)

GOGLIN Christian
Emotions and Values in Equity Crowdfunding Investment Choices 1: Transdisciplinary Theoretical Approach

GUILHON Bernard
Venture Capital and the Financing of Innovation
(Innovation Between Risk and Reward Set – Volume 6)

LATOUCHE Pascal
Open Innovation: Human Set-up
(Innovation and Technology Set – Volume 10)

MAKRIDES Andreas, KARAGRIGORIOU Alex, SKIADAS Christos H.
Data Analysis and Applications 3: Computational, Classification, Financial, Statistical and Stochastic Methods
(Big Data, Artificial Intelligence and Data Analysis Set – Volume 5)
Data Analysis and Applications 4: Financial Data Analysis and Methods
(Big Data, Artificial Intelligence and Data Analysis Set – Volume 6)

MASSOTTE Pierre, CORSI Patrick
Complex Decision-Making in Economy and Finance

MEUNIER François-Xavier
Dual Innovation Systems : Concepts, Tools and Methods
(Smart Innovation Set – Volume 31)

MICHAUD Thomas
Science Fiction and Innovation Design (Innovation in Engineering and Technology Set – Volume 6)

MONINO Jean-Louis
Data Control: Major Challenge for the Digital Society
(Smart Innovation Set – Volume 29)

MORLAT Clément
Sustainable Productive System: Eco-development versus Sustainable Development
(Smart Innovation Set – Volume 26)

SAULAIS Pierre, ERMINE Jean-Louis
Knowledge Management in Innovative Companies 2: Understanding and Deploying a KM Plan within a Learning Organization
(Smart Innovation Set – Volume 27)

2019

AMENDOLA Mario, GAFFARD Jean-Luc
Disorder and Public Concern Around Globalization

BARBAROUX Pierre
Disruptive Technology and Defence Innovation Ecosystems
(Innovation in Engineering and Technology Set – Volume 5)

DOU Henri, JUILLET Alain, CLERC Philippe
Strategic Intelligence for the Future 1: A New Strategic and Operational Approach
Strategic Intelligence for the Future 2: A New Information Function Approach

FRIKHA Azza
Measurement in Marketing: Operationalization of Latent Constructs

FRIMOUSSE Soufyane
Innovation and Agility in the Digital Age
(Human Resources Management Set – Volume 2)

GAY Claudine, SZOSTAK Bérangère L.
Innovation and Creativity in SMEs: Challenges, Evolutions and Prospects
(Smart Innovation Set – Volume 21)

GORIA Stéphane, HUMBERT Pierre, ROUSSEL Benoît
Information, Knowledge and Agile Creativity
(Smart Innovation Set – Volume 22)

HELLER David
Investment Decision-making Using Optional Models
(Economic Growth Set – Volume 2)

HELLER David, DE CHADIRAC Sylvain, HALAOUI Lana, JOUVET Camille
The Emergence of Start-ups
(Economic Growth Set – Volume 1)

HÉRAUD Jean-Alain, KERR Fiona, BURGER-HELMCHEN Thierry
Creative Management of Complex Systems
(Smart Innovation Set – Volume 19)

LATOUCHE Pascal
Open Innovation: Corporate Incubator
(Innovation and Technology Set – Volume 7)

LEHMANN Paul-Jacques
The Future of the Euro Currency

LEIGNEL Jean-Louis, MÉNAGER Emmanuel, YABLONSKY Serge
Sustainable Enterprise Performance: A Comprehensive Evaluation Method

LIÈVRE Pascal, AUBRY Monique, GAREL Gilles
Management of Extreme Situations: From Polar Expeditions to Exploration-Oriented Organizations

MILLOT Michel
Embarrassment of Product Choices 2: Towards a Society of Well-being

N'GOALA Gilles, PEZ-PÉRARD Virginie, PRIM-ALLAZ Isabelle
Augmented Customer Strategy: CRM in the Digital Age

NIKOLOVA Blagovesta
The RRI Challenge: Responsibilization in a State of Tension with Market Regulation
(Innovation and Responsibility Set – Volume 3)

PELLEGRIN-BOUCHER Estelle, ROY Pierre
Innovation in the Cultural and Creative Industries
(Innovation and Technology Set – Volume 8)

PRIOLON Joël
Financial Markets for Commodities

QUINIOU Matthieu
Blockchain: The Advent of Disintermediation

RAVIX Joël-Thomas, DESCHAMPS Marc
Innovation and Industrial Policies
(Innovation between Risk and Reward Set – Volume 5)

ROGER Alain, VINOT Didier
Skills Management: New Applications, New Questions
(Human Resources Management Set – Volume 1)

SAULAIS Pierre, ERMINE Jean-Louis
Knowledge Management in Innovative Companies 1: Understanding and Deploying a KM Plan within a Learning Organization
(Smart Innovation Set – Volume 23)

SERVAJEAN-HILST Romaric
Co-innovation Dynamics: The Management of Client-Supplier Interactions for Open Innovation
(Smart Innovation Set – Volume 20)

SKIADAS Christos H., BOZEMAN James R.
Data Analysis and Applications 1: Clustering and Regression, Modeling-estimating, Forecasting and Data Mining
(Big Data, Artificial Intelligence and Data Analysis Set – Volume 2)
Data Analysis and Applications 2: Utilization of Results in Europe and Other Topics
(Big Data, Artificial Intelligence and Data Analysis Set – Volume 3)

UZUNIDIS Dimitri
Systemic Innovation: Entrepreneurial Strategies and Market Dynamics

VIGEZZI Michel
World Industrialization: Shared Inventions, Competitive Innovations and Social Dynamics
(Smart Innovation Set – Volume 24)

2018

BURKHARDT Kirsten
Private Equity Firms: Their Role in the Formation of Strategic Alliances

CALLENS Stéphane
Creative Globalization
(Smart Innovation Set – Volume 16)

CASADELLA Vanessa
Innovation Systems in Emerging Economies: MINT – Mexico, Indonesia, Nigeria, Turkey
(Smart Innovation Set – Volume 18)

CHOUTEAU Marianne, FOREST Joëlle, NGUYEN Céline
Science, Technology and Innovation Culture
(Innovation in Engineering and Technology Set – Volume 3)

CORLOSQUET-HABART Marine, JANSSEN Jacques
Big Data for Insurance Companies
(Big Data, Artificial Intelligence and Data Analysis Set – Volume 1)

CROS Françoise
Innovation and Society
(Smart Innovation Set – Volume 15)

DEBREF Romain
Environmental Innovation and Ecodesign: Certainties and Controversies
(Smart Innovation Set – Volume 17)

DOMINGUEZ Noémie
SME Internationalization Strategies: Innovation to Conquer New Markets

ERMINE Jean-Louis
Knowledge Management: The Creative Loop
(Innovation and Technology Set – Volume 5)

GILBERT Patrick, BOBADILLA Natalia, GASTALDI Lise,
LE BOULAIRE Martine, LELEBINA Olga
Innovation, Research and Development Management

IBRAHIMI Mohammed
Mergers & Acquisitions: Theory, Strategy, Finance

LEMAÎTRE Denis
Training Engineers for Innovation

LÉVY Aldo, BEN BOUHENI Faten, AMMI Chantal
Financial Management: USGAAP and IFRS Standards
(Innovation and Technology Set – Volume 6)

MILLOT Michel
Embarrassment of Product Choices 1: How to Consume Differently

PANSERA Mario, OWEN Richard
Innovation and Development: The Politics at the Bottom of the Pyramid
(Innovation and Responsibility Set – Volume 2)

RICHEZ Yves
Corporate Talent Detection and Development

SACHETTI Philippe, ZUPPINGER Thibaud
New Technologies and Branding
(Innovation and Technology Set – Volume 4)

SAMIER Henri
Intuition, Creativity, Innovation

TEMPLE Ludovic, COMPAORÉ SAWADOGO Eveline M.F.W.
Innovation Processes in Agro-Ecological Transitions in Developing Countries
(Innovation in Engineering and Technology Set – Volume 2)

UZUNIDIS Dimitri
Collective Innovation Processes: Principles and Practices
(Innovation in Engineering and Technology Set – Volume 4)

VAN HOOREBEKE Delphine
The Management of Living Beings or Emo-management

2017

AÏT-EL-HADJ Smaïl
The Ongoing Technological System
(Smart Innovation Set – Volume 11)

BAUDRY Marc, DUMONT Béatrice
Patents: Prompting or Restricting Innovation?
(Smart Innovation Set – Volume 12)

BÉRARD Céline, TEYSSIER Christine
Risk Management: Lever for SME Development and Stakeholder Value Creation

CHALENÇON Ludivine
Location Strategies and Value Creation of International Mergers and Acquisitions

CHAUVEL Danièle, BORZILLO Stefano
The Innovative Company: An Ill-defined Object
(Innovation between Risk and Reward Set – Volume 1)

CORSI Patrick
Going Past Limits To Growth

D'ANDRIA Aude, GABARRET Inés
Building 21st Century Entrepreneurship
(Innovation and Technology Set – Volume 2)

DAIDJ Nabyla
Cooperation, Coopetition and Innovation
(Innovation and Technology Set – Volume 3)

FERNEZ-WALCH Sandrine
The Multiple Facets of Innovation Project Management
(Innovation between Risk and Reward Set – Volume 4)

FOREST Joëlle
Creative Rationality and Innovation
(Smart Innovation Set – Volume 14)

GUILHON Bernard
Innovation and Production Ecosystems
(Innovation between Risk and Reward Set – Volume 2)

HAMMOUDI Abdelhakim, DAIDJ Nabyla
Game Theory Approach to Managerial Strategies and Value Creation
(Diverse and Global Perspectives on Value Creation Set – Volume 3)

LALLEMENT Rémi
Intellectual Property and Innovation Protection: New Practices and New Policy Issues
(Innovation between Risk and Reward Set – Volume 3)

LAPERCHE Blandine
Enterprise Knowledge Capital
(Smart Innovation Set – Volume 13)

LEBERT Didier, EL YOUNSI Hafida
International Specialization Dynamics
(Smart Innovation Set – Volume 9)

MAESSCHALCK Marc
Reflexive Governance for Research and Innovative Knowledge
(Responsible Research and Innovation Set – Volume 6)

MASSOTTE Pierre
Ethics in Social Networking and Business 1: Theory, Practice and Current Recommendations
Ethics in Social Networking and Business 2: The Future and Changing Paradigms

MASSOTTE Pierre, CORSI Patrick
Smart Decisions in Complex Systems

MEDINA Mercedes, HERRERO Mónica, URGELLÉS Alicia
Current and Emerging Issues in the Audiovisual Industry
(Diverse and Global Perspectives on Value Creation Set – Volume 1)

MICHAUD Thomas
Innovation, Between Science and Science Fiction
(Smart Innovation Set – Volume 10)

PELLÉ Sophie
Business, Innovation and Responsibility
(Responsible Research and Innovation Set – Volume 7)

SAVIGNAC Emmanuelle
The Gamification of Work: The Use of Games in the Workplace

SUGAHARA Satoshi, DAIDJ Nabyla, USHIO Sumitaka
Value Creation in Management Accounting and Strategic Management: An Integrated Approach
(Diverse and Global Perspectives on Value Creation Set –Volume 2)

UZUNIDIS Dimitri, SAULAIS Pierre
Innovation Engines: Entrepreneurs and Enterprises in a Turbulent World
(Innovation in Engineering and Technology Set – Volume 1)

2016

BARBAROUX Pierre, ATTOUR Amel, SCHENK Eric
Knowledge Management and Innovation
(Smart Innovation Set – Volume 6)

BEN BOUHENI Faten, AMMI Chantal, LEVY Aldo
Banking Governance, Performance And Risk-Taking: Conventional Banks Vs Islamic Banks

BOUTILLIER Sophie, CARRÉ Denis, LEVRATTO Nadine
Entrepreneurial Ecosystems (Smart Innovation Set – Volume 2)

BOUTILLIER Sophie, UZUNIDIS Dimitri
The Entrepreneur (Smart Innovation Set – Volume 8)

BOUVARD Patricia, SUZANNE Hervé
Collective Intelligence Development in Business

GALLAUD Delphine, LAPERCHE Blandine
Circular Economy, Industrial Ecology and Short Supply Chains (Smart Innovation Set – Volume 4)

GUERRIER Claudine
Security and Privacy in the Digital Era (Innovation and Technology Set – Volume 1)

MEGHOUAR Hicham
Corporate Takeover Targets

MONINO Jean-Louis, SEDKAOUI Soraya
Big Data, Open Data and Data Development (Smart Innovation Set – Volume 3)

MOREL Laure, LE ROUX Serge
Fab Labs: Innovative User (Smart Innovation Set – Volume 5)

PICARD Fabienne, TANGUY Corinne
Innovations and Techno-ecological Transition (Smart Innovation Set – Volume 7)

2015

CASADELLA Vanessa, LIU Zeting, DIMITRI Uzunidis
Innovation Capabilities and Economic Development in Open Economies (Smart Innovation Set – Volume 1)

CORSI Patrick, MORIN Dominique
Sequencing Apple's DNA

CORSI Patrick, NEAU Erwan
Innovation Capability Maturity Model

FAIVRE-TAVIGNOT Bénédicte
Social Business and Base of the Pyramid

GODÉ Cécile
Team Coordination in Extreme Environments

MAILLARD Pierre
Competitive Quality and Innovation

MASSOTTE Pierre, CORSI Patrick
Operationalizing Sustainability

MASSOTTE Pierre, CORSI Patrick
Sustainability Calling

2014

DUBÉ Jean, LEGROS Diègo
Spatial Econometrics Using Microdata

LESCA Humbert, LESCA Nicolas
Strategic Decisions and Weak Signals

2013

HABART-CORLOSQUET Marine, JANSSEN Jacques, MANCA Raimondo
VaR Methodology for Non-Gaussian Finance

2012

DAL PONT Jean-Pierre
Process Engineering and Industrial Management

MAILLARD Pierre
Competitive Quality Strategies

POMEROL Jean-Charles
Decision-Making and Action

SZYLAR Christian
UCITS Handbook

2011

LESCA Nicolas
Environmental Scanning and Sustainable Development

LESCA Nicolas, LESCA Humbert
Weak Signals for Strategic Intelligence: Anticipation Tool for Managers

MERCIER-LAURENT Eunika
Innovation Ecosystems

2010

SZYLAR Christian
Risk Management under UCITS III/IV

2009

COHEN Corine
Business Intelligence

ZANINETTI Jean-Marc
Sustainable Development in the USA

2008

CORSI Patrick, DULIEU Mike
The Marketing of Technology Intensive Products and Services

DZEVER Sam, JAUSSAUD Jacques, ANDREOSSO Bernadette
Evolving Corporate Structures and Cultures in Asia: Impact of Globalization

2007

AMMI Chantal
Global Consumer Behavior

2006

BOUGHZALA Imed, ERMINE Jean-Louis
Trends in Enterprise Knowledge Management

CORSI Patrick *et al.*
Innovation Engineering: the Power of Intangible Networks